THE PRACTICE OF MEDITATION

THE PRACTICE
OF MEDITATION

by

KLEMENS TILMANN

Paulist Press

First published in Great Britain by Search Press
Limited, 2-10 Jerdan Place, London SW6 5PT.

Published originally under the title ÜBUNGSBUCH
ZUR MEDITATION by Benziger Verlag, Zürich,
Switzerland.

Translated from the German by
David Smith.

ISBN: 0-8091-2043-7

Library of Congress
Catalog Card Number: 77-72469

Published in the U.S.A. by Paulist Press
Editorial Office: 1865 Broadway, N.Y., N.Y. 10023
Business Office: 545 Island Road, Ramsey, N.J. 07446

Printed and bound in the U.S.A.

CONTENTS

Part I: General exercises and materials

Part III: Christian meditations

Full lotus

Half-lotus

Sitting on a stool

Sitting on one's heels (front view)

Sitting on one's heels (rear view)

Sitting on one's heels with support

Saddle position

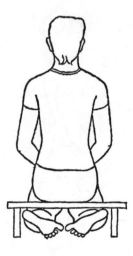

Sitting on a low bench

FOREWORD

People today feel a deep need for meditation. They know they are in danger of losing everything that is real and valuable in their lives in the bustle, pressure and tension of the modern world. They know the threat of inward frustration. They know this quite irrespective of philosophy or religion, and they long to experience life at a deeper level.

This need for meditation is often accompanied by a deep questioning and a desire to understand the meaning of such realities as life, the growth towards maturity, love, death and fulfilment. Many people want above all to 'have life and have it abundantly'. They are looking for the ultimate and all-embracing reality of God. They long to live in God. I have written this book for people like that.

I have tried to offer a series of models as a basis for continued meditation, rather than a snap course.

Some readers will be old, others young; some married, others single. There will be beginners, as well as those who, through daily practice, have advanced further in meditation. Some will still be seeking faith, whereas others will have reached a certain maturity.

I have tried to graduate and diversify the models in this book and to provide material ranging from the most fundamental, accessible to anybody, to the more advanced that will be of help to those who are more spiritually mature. First select the exercises that you find most helpful.

But all those who use this book have one fundamental thing in common—all are human, and one of the essential reasons for meditation is to become more human. The fact that there are so many different kinds of model and exercise in the book should lead all readers, whatever their stage of development, to the very heart of meditation, so long as they do not pass over what is essential and original in themselves, but try consciously to reach it. Meditation is, after all, not like snow, which conceals the field with a white, clean covering. It is more like the spring, which allows the field to come to full life.

This book does not provide a closed system of meditation. Unless the reader meditates on his own initiative, he will probably not be able to penetrate very far into the depths of his own being. If, on the other hand, he discovers what is essential in himself after suitable instruction, he should make progress.

This book ought to help satisfy a need which is urgent, and of permanent human value. It should fulfil a need which goes to the very heart of life. It ought to help us to become full of the living breath of meditation at the deepest level of our being.

TWELVE BASIC RULES

1.   Do not be deterred by the great diversity of material offered in this book. Do not spend too much time sampling. Make up your mind, choose something and stick to it.

2.   Practise regularly. At least ten to twenty minutes a day for five days a week and twice a week at least a little longer.

3.   Never practise half-heartedly. Always take care that you will not be disturbed during meditation and that you are in the right physical position, motionless and breathing correctly, so that you will be perfectly at peace and able to meditate at depth.

4.   The 'fundamental exercise' and the 'I am here' exercise may provide sufficient material for some time. These exercises have no object in view and lead directly into experience in depth. They can and ought to be used again and again, sometimes on their own and sometimes to introduce meditation with an object.

5.   It is better to repeat one exercise and the material in it than to be constantly in search of new material. Many of the exercises call for frequent repetition.

6.   Before you begin any exercise, be sure of what you are going to practise. It is best to make sure of this on the previous day. Turn over in your mind occasionally what material you intend to use in the days ahead.

7.   Begin sometimes at the point where you left off the day

before. Go back into the same meditation and allow it to develop further.

8. If you use a text for meditation, cover everything else, including any other parts of the same text, with white paper, so that only the selected text is visible. In this way, there will be no distractions and your text will be effective. The same applies to any picture used for meditation.

9. If the object is something concrete and perceptible, you must begin by a thorough perception of the whole object. Do not be satisfied with a generalized 'Oh, I know that already'. You must experience the object in its originality.

10. Keep to the 'bowl movement' when no other procedures follow—after perceiving the entire object, move from outside and above to the innermost and deepest level, from the many to the few, to the simplest, to the one and to the ultimate, and stay there. Let the ultimate reality come to you and speak to you. Move from active doing to passive receiving, from standing over and against to becoming one.

11. Keep as close as you can in your everyday life to the basic attitude of meditation, depending, of course, on what you are doing at the time. Be alert to all experiences which cause you to wonder or to begin to meditate spontaneously. When you are faced with a period of intense professional activity, be sure to cease meditating well beforehand and to remain in a state of *hara*, so as to be able to devote yourself entirely to the activity that lies ahead. Afterwards, make use of the freedom to return quickly to a state of peace.

12. Any meditation in which you are seeking God must be fulfilled life and not simply an opportunity to perform an exercise. Even silent peace spent with God is prayer. It is, however, a good practice to conclude such interior experience with a verbal prayer.

THE PRACTICE OF MEDITATION

1.   *Reading and underlining*
The first thing you will want to do with this book is, of course, to
find out what it contains. You will go through it and read it. You
should not, however, be content to leave it at that. When you read
it, underline anything that promises to be rewarding and draws you
down to a deeper level. You could perhaps mark such passages with
an 'M' (for meditation) and use them more intensively in the exercises as they occur.
   It is most important to avoid simply reading the pages that follow,
above all if they seem to point to a deeper experience. Our aim is to
meditate, but we are always so quick to set this aside and replace
meditation by an easier activity.

2.   *Differences between texts*

If an exercise in this book is described as a text for 'guidance',
keep the text in front of you during the exercise. Whenever you
come to three dots in the text, turn your eyes away from the text
and let the inner procedure take its own course. As soon as this
procedure begins to fade, look at the text again. In group meditation, a text for guidance can be read aloud, after an introduction
such as 'I am here', by a member of the group, slowly, expressively
and with suitable pauses (indicated by the dots). (A tape recorder
can be used here. A tape can be previously prepared with the text
spoken in this way and allowed to play or be switched off at suitable
points during the exercise.)
   If an exercise is marked 'leading to meditation', the text should
be read, carefully considered and then set aside. Pure inner meditation should then follow.
   A 'testimony' does not lead directly to meditation. It does no
more than provide an idea for an inner procedure. The reader
knows that this is what happened in the case of another person and

what is said in the testimony may be infectious and stimulate him. It may act as a model or as a 'leading' text, but it should not alienate him. It should stir up his own original thoughts and help him to meditate in his own deep and personal way.

3. Spend some time on the exercises in part one

If you do not, you will find that, when you do the exercises in the second part of the book, they have insufficient contact with reality and become a question of reading and reflection or else a pure exertion of your will.

4. Do not just practise alone

It is a good plan to meet at least once a month with others as a group, in order to practise meditation together and exchange experiences (relaxation, basic exercises, statement of themes and 'leading' texts, questions and clarifications). You can also begin the 'bowl movement' within a group framework. This is always easier if one of the members leads the others, by means of previously prepared questions, to the object in view. Such questions, for example, as: What do I perceive? To what sphere does the object belong? What does it mean to us? What can it signify for us? The content and meaning of these questions will differ according to the material under consideration. I have already mentioned the value of reading aloud a text for guidance in a slow, expressive voice and it is also valuable to hold a discussion within the context of a text for instruction. It is important, however, not to allow this discussion to become a rational argument.

It is an excellent practice to consult an expert two or three times a year (to discuss with him the nature of the exercises followed, any difficulties encountered, positive effects or progress made and any questions that have arisen). For this reason, keep notes in the form of a diary.

5. Patience

The process of growth towards maturity in meditation will be a long one. Certain elements may come quite quickly—greater peace, a taste for experience in depth, a contact with people and things at the level of reality and a joyful experience of life with God.

Other elements, however, will only be accessible after years of practice, when one is in one's sixties, and even then the end will not have been reached. Endless life beckons. Have patience. Go forward step by step. Keep on the path. Do not be discouraged by setbacks—begin again.

SOME WORDS EXPLAINED

Hara is a Japanese word meaning belly. In its extended sense, it means a total disposition of the body and soul together, in which the belly is seen as the centre of gravity in the person meditating. In hara, the upper forces are relaxed and a healing effect can be exerted from the depth of the person's being. The whole person is in a state of profound recollection and is open to receive the deepest experience and the ultimate mystery of life. In any course of meditation, we are taught how to practise hara and the more we meditate, the more it increases and the more it becomes part of our constant disposition. It is an indispensable prerequisite for meditation in depth and at the same time the fruit of that meditation. Hara could perhaps be translated as the centre of one's physical and spiritual being

Two other terms used in this book, to 'interiorize' and 'interior experience', are to some extent synonymous with to 'meditate' and 'meditation', but they cover a much wider spectrum and include such ideas as considering, musing, pondering, reflection, taking to heart and even 'tasting'.

Meditation is a process that takes place in the most interior part of our innermost being and when we meditate we are recollected and peaceful and at the deepest level of our existence. Anyone who has never experienced meditation does not understand what it is. It is too profound to be understood rationally, intellectually or analytically and it cannot be achieved by a determined act of the will. We can and must prepare ourselves for it, but it has to come of itself, like sleep or a conscientious decision. But surely we all used to meditate when we were children, completely lost in play or listening to a story. Meditation may take many forms and can take place at different levels. What is essential is that we cease to be active in thinking or doing and become receptive. When this happens, we no longer examine a thing, for example, or a picture or a text, but the object, the picture or the text becomes active in us and says something to us. The basic exercise and the 'I am here' exercise (pp. 20-22) are both very helpful in leading us to that kind of meditation.

The meaning of the word meditation has changed. In the past, a distinction was made between three stages in the spiritual life. The first of these was known as 'reading' (*lectio*). In the second stage of meditation proper or consideration (*meditatio*), the object was actively presented to the mind, considered and elaborated. It was in the third stage of *contemplatio* or seeing that one achieved a deep inner peace and was fully receptive. Nowadays, probably because we have been influenced by eastern thinking, we understand meditation in the third sense in which I have described it above.

Many people are looking for meditation now because they have lost or are losing the depth and the centre of their being, what is most real to them, in the noise, haste and superficiality of modern existence. They long to find that centre again in order to be fully human.

Meditation is simple and in some respects childishly easy—all normal children meditate, at least until they are about ten. Yet at the same time anyone who wants to find meditation and reach maturity in it must be prepared to follow a long path. Along this path, we are cured and made whole and we continue to grow towards maturity as long as we live, however old we become. Meditation is the highway to God and the way along which we are perfected in faith and love.

By 'the bowl', we mean the movement in meditation in which we press forward in a reality from outside to within, that is, from what can be experienced externally to the central mystery within, and at the same time move from above to below, that is, from the surface to the depth. This movement from outside and above to within and below resembles a bowl, which is shaped from the outside upper edge to the centre and the depth. A similar movement also takes place in meditation inside the person meditating. He moves from an external and more superficial attitude to a state of recollection, inwardness and profound experience.

Various terms are used to describe the path to meditation and its course—seeing, observing, total perception, reflection, assimilation, comparing and relating, penetration, allowing the object to have an effect on oneself, tasting and staying or repose.

Diaphragm breathing is the natural way of breathing that we had when we were children. It brings a deep peace and recollectedness. Many of us have come to breathe at the level of the chest, in this way expressing our determination, our agitation, our self-assertion and our will to succeed. In this kind of breathing, our ribs are always in motion, so that we always depend on the help of our muscles. In any course in meditation, we have to learn how to breathe from the diaphragm. Anyone who wants to learn diaphragm breathing on his own should make use of the following exercises.

Lie stretched out on your back on the floor. Let your hands move down over your shoulders to your shoulder-blades. Draw up your feet to that your knees are raised, cross one foot over the other and let your knees fall apart. If you place a book on your belly while you are in this position, it will move up and down, because you will be breathing from the diaphragm. Become conscious of this kind of breathing and try to encourage it in daily exercises so that it becomes part of your everyday life.

In the second of these exercises, kneel on the floor and sit on your heels. Now lean forward and place your forehead on the floor. Grasp your hips with both hands, keeping your fingers pointing backwards. You will feel yourself breathing from the diaphragm. This breathing must become your natural breathing.

PART I

GENERAL EXERCISES AND MATERIALS

I BASIC EXERCISES

1. Elements of the exercises

(a) Positions

Half-lotus: take off your shoes, sit on a small cushion or folded blanket and draw your left leg right up so that your heel is in your crotch. Now draw up your right leg and place the foot with the sole facing upwards on the left side. Put your hands one inside the other in the form of a bowl, leaving the thumbs free to move and with the outer edges of the hands on the abdomen. Straighten the upper part of the body and then, without bending your back, let it sink into the pelvis. Sit upright and do not bend the head forward. Keep your nose central, above the navel (see p. 5).

Full lotus and sitting on a stool: (see pp. 5 & 6).

Sitting on one's heels: kneel on a blanket without shoes, the tips of the big toes touching and the heels outwards. Now sit on your heels (see pp. 6 & 7).

Easier positions for older people: to avoid tension in the knees and ankles, place a rolled blanket or small bolster under the buttocks and the ankles (see p. 7). For the saddle position see p. 8. A low bench can also be used (see p. 8).

(b) Lowering of the inner centre of gravity (Hara exercise)

Let the inner centre of gravity fall slowly from your head through your body into the lower part of your body between your navel and your hands, and thus achieve hara.

(c) Diaphragm breathing

Practise this first as a separate exercise, then use it consciously during mechanical tasks, until you do it without thinking, like speaking.

(d) The four beats in breathing

In the fundamental exercise, breathe out — breathe out — pause — breathe in.

(e) The words accompanying these beats

Let go — sink down — become one — become new (or, at the beginning: let come).

(f) At the beginning and end of each exercise

Make a deep obeisance. This will help you to achieve the proper disposition and to express reverence or thankfulness.

2. The fundamental exercise

Begin by sitting in the right position, then go on to diaphragm breathing, saying the words: 'let go — sink down — become one — let come'. While you are saying them, let them be expressed inwardly or rather simply let what they express happen. Sink lower and lower and let go of everything that you want, are thinking about or aim to achieve, and above all of yourself. Sink down into your own inward depths, to the lowest point of your being. Become one with your own depths, the centre of gravity in the lower part of your body, the lowest point of your being, which will gradually become open to the ultimate ground of all being. You will then enter hara. Now let your breath come (do not breathe deliberately). By this fourth beat in the bar of breathing, you will be growing more and more peaceful, going deeper and deeper and becoming new. This fundamental exercise thus becomes a 'wheel of change' and of its own accord reaches a deeper and deeper level.

3. The 'I am here' exercise — A text for guidance

The following model ought, if it is combined with a correct position of the body and diaphragm breathing, to help you acquire the basic spiritual disposition that is necessary for meditation. The last sections, if carried out correctly, can also be used for meditation as such. This exercise can and should be repeated frequently, leaving out certain passages and emphasizing others as required.

(a) I reach peace . . . Everything passes . . . like the rippling on a peaceful lake when a stone is thrown into the water . . . moving further and further away . . . becoming smoother and smoother . . . Then the water becomes motionless and peaceful . . . I . . . am . . . completely . . . at peace . . .

(b) I have time . . . Nothing is urgent . . . I have freedom from everything . . . Time is standing still . . . like a great bell suspended in the air above me . . .

(c) I remain undisturbed in a space of freedom . . . I am released from everything . . . What existed previously is far away . . . shut out, as it were by a thick padded door . . . What is still to come is also far away . . . unattainable, excluded by a door . . . In this room of freedom I am undisturbed . . . I can be completely myself . . . I enjoy it . . . (Nor do the people near me disturb me . . . like me, they are looking for silence . . . they help me by their peace . . .)

(d) I am quite recollected . . . there is nothing outside . . . Every thought has been brought into this room . . . with me . . . in me . . . More and more I come to myself . . . not concentrated – that would be the result of my own will . . . but released . . . peacefully everything is collected and recollected in me . . . more and more I am with myself . . . in my body . . . in my depth . . .

(e) I am relaxed and released . . . I let everything go . . . my forehead is relaxed and smooth . . . no creases between the eyebrows and no wrinkles above them . . . as though a loving hand had smoothed them out . . . I let everything go . . . my eyes . . . my cheeks . . . I feel them hanging lightly . . . I let my jaws and mouth go . . . My face is no longer severe . . . no longer serious, but smiling . . . I let my shoulders go . . . the right upper arm . . . I feel the muscles hanging lightly . . . I let my forearm go . . . my right hand . . . my left arm . . . Everything is relaxed and released . . . my chest . . .

belly . . . hips . . . the lower part of my body . . . pelvis . . . buttocks
. . . thighs . . . the muscles are hanging and relaxed . . . calves . . .
feet . . . toes . . . everything is relaxed and released.
I let myself go spiritually. Nothing is pressing on me . . . no worry . . .
no care . . . no exertion of the will . . . no sense of duty . . . no
mask . . . I do not want to hold on to myself . . . to preserve myself . . . present an image of myself . . . I let myself go completely . . .
I let my breath go . . . wherever it likes . . . Now I have let everything that is in me go . . . everything is relaxed . . . released.

(f)   I am entirely present . . . My body is here . . . I have passed
straight through it . . . I can feel it . . . present at the same time in
all its parts . . .
My whole being is present, not only my body . . . I am present . . .
I, this unique being . . . as a man, as a woman . . . I am present
with all my gifts . . . with my whole history as a man, as a woman
. . . with everything that I have ever experienced . . . with everything that is in me (what I have achieved . . . what I failed to do . . .)
with all my desires . . . with all my intentions . . . with all my possibilities . . . with all my riches . . . the whole of me . . .
My depth is present . . . not only the little part of it that I know . . .
I am more and more present with my depth . . . with my whole,
unfathomable depth . . .
(I am present with my roots in the whole of creation . . . in the
people I know . . . in God . . . I am rooted in creation . . . it flows,
into me . . .)
I am present with all this . . . I am not sleepy, but wide awake and
fresh . . . open and ready . . . I am full . . .

(g)   I remain full. Nothing is absent . . . Nothing is pushed out . . .
I . . . am . . . completely present . . . I . . . am . . . completely . . .
here . . . It is very beautiful . . .
I am quite full . . . I accept it completely . . . I remain full.

4. Meditation has a positive aim

We can only accept what is good and healing into the most interior part of our innermost being. Only what is positive can nourish us. What is negative can only destroy our inner life. We do not overlook this negative aspect. We reflect about it, consider it and try to estimate its extent. We think what we can do to overcome it. Above all, however, we avoid becoming one with it. Meditation has a positive aim. It is directed towards positive values and, in the end, towards the ultimate value.

It is often the negative aspect that affects us most. It is disturbing. Many people can only think critically and often only negatively. It is possible that they may also try to excuse themselves by the presence of that negative aspect.

That is why it is a basic experience for many of us to meditate — because meditation above all has a positive aim. Meditation is an exercise and in it we practise again and again our ability to see what is valuable, right, beautiful, good and healing, essential, refreshing, strengthening and edifying. It is only if we aim at and achieve what is positive that the ultimate value and ultimate being will become visible. If we do not train ourselves to set aside our deficiencies and all that is lacking around us and to see what is positive, we shall never escape from critical thinking (this is, of course, necessary, but not at all times) and go to a deeper level of experience. We shall never learn how to meditate about anything human, which of course always has a negative aspect, or indeed anything natural.

If we train ourselves to become positive, we shall also overcome any negative disposition that remains in us. And the person who aims to meditate must certainly overcome any tendency to be dissatisfied, negatively critical and closed to what is good and creative in life.

II   TOTAL PERCEPTION

This is something that is bound to precede meditation, to bring us close to it or even to lead us directly into it. Let us give a few examples which may enable the reader to discover this for himself: horse-chestnut trees in flower tossed by the wind — a field full of flowers,

many-coloured, many different shapes — a forest — a distant landscape — snow driven by the wind — daybreak — dusk — children
building sandcastles on the beach — people who are close to us in
life and work. The most important examples, however, are naturally
those about which we want to meditate.

III   DO EVERYTHING TOTALLY

A disciple in the art of meditation once complained to his master
that he could never find time to meditate. The master replied:
'Everything that you do, do totally. If you are reading, read totally.
If you are with your wife, be with her totally. If you are playing
with your children, be totally with them in the game. When you
eat, eat as though you were receiving a total gift. Whenever you are
talking to someone, be with him totally, listening and giving. Give
yourself totally to everything you do — working and sleeping, in
your leisure time and in prayer. If you do this, you will find your
way into the depths of meditation in the middle of life.'

There are many aspects of our ordinary, everyday lives which
can provide us with an opportunity to meditate. The more we
live in a state of hara, the easier it will be to perform all our activities totally and to be totally immersed in them.

IV   SELF-ACCEPTANCE — A TEXT FOR GUIDANCE

The following text expresses a fundamental act of human existence.
It should arouse in us certain essential elements in the practice of
meditation, making us, for example, sober and truthful, courageous
and selfless and enabling us boldly to confront the ultimate reality
and in the end to give ourselves entirely to the one who is waiting
to give to us. We shall be able to accept ourselves entirely, not when
we obtain control of our own wills, but only when we learn how to

penetrate, in complete freedom and without any external pressure, into the most hidden recesses of our innermost selves and in this way break down all inner resistance.

The five sets of material that follow are arranged in five days, but this does not mean that they have to be covered in exactly this time. You should spend as long as you think it is necessary to spend on each one and do what seems to you to be important. Above all, you should not remain in a state of generalized thoughts and good, but vague intentions. You should resolve to make everything that is general particular and everything that is vague concrete in your life.

1. First day: I am given to myself

Here, your task should be to let yourself be deeply affected, even shaken by this unalterable fact and this powerful reality; namely, that you are given to yourself, and, having considered it carefully, to experience it as intensely as possible in various spheres of your own life. This may perhaps lead to an initial change of attitude.

1. I find myself here

I perceive this realistically in my body — I look at my hand, move it, touch it. I take my head in my hands, feel it. I see and experience the way in which I see and hear, sit, move my arms, breathe . . . I can feel my whole body. I find myself here. I also find my inner being here. I say: 'I'. I think, feel, hope, expect, trust, seek . . . There is no doubt about it. It is an unchangeable fact. I find myself here. Nothing — no dream, no desire, no action — can take this away. I perceive myself in reflection — the whole reality that I find here. The circulation of my blood, respiration and the supply of oxygen to my body, my external and internal organs and their mysterious functioning . . . My capacity for inner experience. What have I experienced in my inner life? Happiness, illusion, joy, disappointment, love, annoyance, self-abandonment, repentance, patience . . . All this I find here.

2. I am unique

I find myself here as this one particular person. Conceived on one particular day, born on another. With this face, this finger-print, this name. Male or female. Coming from this particular family, with this history, this education. With these skills and abilities. With these limitations and inhibitions. With everything that has happened to me and that I have done. In this particular place in the world, at this moment in the history of the world. Dependent on this world, these people, this period in history . . . committed to live within this circle of relationships. I am this unique person.

3. I am here without having been asked

I did not choose to exist. My existence here was given to me. Was it forced on me? If so, by whom? I am here apparently as the result of pure chance — my parents happened to get to know each other, they came together at this moment in time and these cells were united . . . Is that the reason for my being here? If so, is my existence here not simply due to chance? Is it not meaningless? Many people think this and accept an existence that is without reason, an absurdity. Or is the real reason for my existence here to be found at a depth far below that at which ordinary events take place? Does not a great deal that is meaningful in my earlier life point to this? Especially my constant quest for meaning in my life, a search that I cannot give up? If this is so, then I must be here because the real reason for my existence is an ultimate one . . .

4. I am given to myself

It is not just that I find myself here — I am also given to myself in a mysterious way. I have to try to understand this and experience it as a living reality . . . I am myself the material that is available to me, that is given to me. And how rich it is! I know this when I think of all the people in the world who are blind, deaf or crippled, or those who are mentally ill or disturbed. How much has been given to me! How much I possess! And yet I do not possess myself entirely. I still have difficulty in understanding myself, in fathoming my motives, in coming to grips with myself, in becoming truly myself . . . I am given to myself as a mystery. How should I associate with myself? How ought I to live with that mystery?

5. *I am given to myself as a project*

I cannot do what I want to with myself, manipulate myself. I cannot add an organ or a limb to my body. My whole being is designed in a certain way and predisposed towards certain forms. I have to realize this project of myself just as any animal has to fulfil its own essential design. Mine is a spiritual project and, what is more, this particular spiritual project. It is this particular design that has to be accomplished in me. I am designed as a man or as a woman. I can only become myself insofar as I correspond to that design. If I do not accept it as my point of departure, I will mistake my true identity, betray my essential being, become self-contradictory and disrupted, false to myself and self-alienated. I will become a caricature of myself . . . There is only one way to live in health and freedom — I must accept the fact that I am given to myself. The 'material' has been given to me, together with its potential, and I have the power to do something with it.

2. Second day: I am given up to myself

Seize hold of what you have already recognized in a general sense to be a project or design, that is, yourself, and grasp it as a particular reality. Become aware of yourself as a possibility and a task, accept and experience yourself fully and say yes in your innermost self to yourself.

1. *I can do something with my 'material'. With my life*

I can associate properly with it, so that it will prosper and develop properly . . . I can listen attentively to the message that my life is communicating to me, that I need to grow and move forward. I can also set myself worthy aims . . . I can give myself up to something worth while. If I live properly, I will grow towards maturity and become more and more complete . . . I can think calmly about this aim and the way towards it . . . Patiently and consistently I can follow the way step by step . . .

I can do something with my body. Good health is not simply the result of chance. Which aspects of my body ought I to develop, strengthen or exercise? What are my weak spots and how can I overcome them? Which skills ought I to develop? How can I improve my appearance? My body can be controlled. It can also be filled with spirit. I must learn to see, observe and perceive my body . . .

I can also develop my innermost self, set it in order, strengthen it, deepen it, enrich and ennoble it. What would be the best way to do this?

I can do something with my 'material' for the world in which I am living. In this way, I can play a part in making the world a better place. I can do what is within my power to make life better for my fellow men, for children and others in my family, in my work and in all my activities. I can help to overcome evil in the world and to build up a future that is worthy of man . . .

2.   *I shall only be able to do this if I accept myself completely as the person that I am*

I should no longer dream of being someone else . . . I must live as this man, this woman. I must see what is positive in me and accept it entirely as my responsibility. I must calmly and soberly recognize my limitations and learn to get along with them (and not mistakenly regard them as too severe). I must accept my own limitations. I must accept myself as I am now, with my gifts, abilities and strong points and also with my weaknesses and failings — these are, after all, given to me for me to overcome them. I must also accept myself in the different stages of development towards which I am constant- ly impelled by my innermost being and which I have to live through. I must accept myself as a person who is on the way, who is bound to develop more and more and who can only gradually come closer to the ultimate reality. I must accept myself as I find myself here and now and above all as a task.

It is only if I accept myself completely, without illusions, in readiness, bravely and lovingly that I will become free and develop correctly. I am given up to myself.

In the above meditation, our aim is clearly to see everything that is present in our existence and in our inner being and without reservation to say yes to it, both as a gift and as a task.

3. Third day: What makes self-acceptance difficult

There is a great deal in me that prevents me from accepting myself as I am.

1. Desires

It is an essential aspect of our being as men and women that we are in constant movement, desiring, hoping, expecting, aiming at a goal. What do I really want for myself? What is my deepest desire? (I should ask myself this question sincerely again and again, examine myself in detail and write down the answer when I am sure of it.)

Have I any desires which cannot be fulfilled? What are they? Do I want to be someone or something that I cannot be? (Perhaps I even want other people to be what they cannot be?) Are my ideals unrealistic? Do they make too severe demands on me? All desires that cannot be fulfilled are an obstacle to living properly. They divert my 'material' into a blind alley in which everything becomes blocked and congested. They tear me apart and paralyze my inner being . . . They prevent me from going freely along the right path, from achieving what is possible, from doing what is within my capacity to do and from accomplishing the task that I am. They crush me and dissipate my powers.

I must learn to do without everything that cannot be fulfilled . . . I will try, carefully, honestly and consistently to do without. This may only be possible if I learn to begin anew again and again. To do without and to abandon desires and ideals which are unattainable is seldom easy, but always necessary. What is more, it will set me free.

2. Shortcomings, limitations and failures that prevent me from accepting myself

There is much in my character that I cannot like. I can hardly bear to acknowledge the existence of these faults. They are unpleasant aspects of myself that I would prefer not to exist.

(a) I must patiently and openly allow those aspects of myself that I would like to repress to be expressed. They include certain facial expressions, habits, inner difficulties, limitations and absences in myself of qualities for which I envy other people.

(b) I must honestly confess to myself that it is not easy to accept these failings.

(c) I must also, however, not accept those failings which can and should be changed. In such cases, acceptance means regarding these curable faults as a task and trying to overcome them.

3. Trouble

It is also sometimes difficult to accept what is positive in myself, because every gift imposes a responsibility on me and I am bound to develop it, exercise it gently and patiently, fashion it and allow it to bear fruit for others. My gifts are not there simply for me. They are given to me for others. There is a form of inertia and self-satisfaction which makes acceptance difficult. Is this the case with me? If it is, then I must clearly acknowledge it and overcome it. (Our task at this stage is to defy all inner resistance and courageously, humbly, freely and fully to say yes to ourselves. We may find it easier to do this by saying 'I am myself' and 'I want to be myself' at the deepest possible level and for as long as necessary, until what was said has been achieved. In the following section, this task is discussed in greater detail.

It is, of course, almost impossible for most of us to know ourselves without consulting another person. For this reason, it is, at this stage, worth going to someone else whom one trusts and by whom one is accepted and loved. This person could be asked to go through the text of the third day in a helpful, positive and entirely open way. He could then point out your strengths on the one hand and your weaknesses on the other.

4. Fourth day: What makes self-acceptance easy

We have to be inwardly impelled to express what is of fundamental importance to our existence. We can be helped in this by considering five aspects of our inner nature.

1. *Deep desires arising from our inner being*

I must let these desires arise freely. Above all, the desire to be made whole and to live rightly and the desire to be free, to have control over myself and to assert myself and to make something of myself and my life. These desires impel me to say Yes to myself.

2. *The knowledge that it is right for me to accept myself*

To reject myself is not a sign of maturity or a balanced attitude. It is a sign of inner resistance and is meaningless. Self-rejection makes me inhibited, deprives me of my inner freedom, ties me up in contradictions, restricts my life and makes me appear to others as immature, unbalanced and failing. I must know myself and accept myself. It is meaningless to oppose what cannot be changed in myself or to cling to wishes that cannot be fulfilled.

3. *A knowledge of my positive potential*

What possibilities for good are there in me? What can I do that will benefit my fellow-men? What contribution can I make to society and what tasks can I undertake – tasks that others may not undertake or will perhaps not do so well?

4. *Looking below me*

There are people whose personalities are much more difficult than mine, people who are less gifted and less likeable. But these people also have to accept themselves and make what they can of their lives. Perhaps I am really quite high up the ladder.

5. *Looking back at my origin*

(a) Looking into the depth of my being. The most important question in my life is what is its meaning? Does my existence depend on pure chance? Is it merely the union of a male and a female cell? Is that the only reason for my being here? The questioning goes even deeper, down to the depths of all being, the ground from which everything comes and on which everything is based, the ultimate ground of all being, the mystery of the world.

(b) In the light of revelation, I came into being because God wanted it.
He called me into being. He was and is behind everything that
caused me to be. I was produced by his love. He has said: 'I have
loved you with an everlasting love' (Jer 31. 3). The living God knows
me. He knows my limitations and my potential. Above all, he says
yes to me. He wants me to live. He stands behind my being, my
being here as I am. He wants me to be made whole. He loves me, has
led me to where I am now and he continues to fashion me. He
accepts me as I am. Why, then, should I not be able to accept
myself?

5. Fifth day: Self-acceptance

1. I am confronted with the facts of my own being, my own history
and my present condition. I do not intend to put up with what is
undesirable in my being or apparently unchangeable. These aspects
of my life have been given to me by God as a task, so that, in over-
coming them and learning self-control, I can grow to maturity.
For this reason, then, I accept them and give myself over entirely
to his will. In this way, I shall find peace.

2. With my whole being, I say yes to him, both in his height and in
his depth. I accept him as my friend and say to him: 'We must
learn to live together. We will stay together and help each other.
We will make the best possible use of each other. We will become
perfectly one . . .'

3. I accept myself as given by God. I am given to you. I come
from your love. I do not understand everything involved in this
gift of myself, but accept that you give me to myself. I am given to
myself. I am given as a many-sided gift and as a many-sided task.
In return, I give myself up to you and ask you to do what, in love,
you wish to do with me. I want to be your instrument and to
carry out what you have in mind for me. I accept myself and trust
that you will be with me. Courageously, patiently and in humility,
I say Yes to you.
    In accepting myself, I also accept you, your will for me and

your love for me. I can easily accept your love and accept it fully. In saying yes to you from the depth of my being, I am set free. At the same time, I also say Yes to myself.

(The whole of this text can best be concluded in dialogue with God himself.)

V   YOUR OWN LIFE
TEXTS LEADING TO MEDITATION

The following instructions may be helpful in deepening your interior experience of your own life.

1. Your own experience

Do not attempt to repress this experience. Let it remain present within you. Accept it. Let it speak to you. Let it tell you what it has to tell you. Then go on to think what you can possibly do about it.

2. Retrospective meditations

In these meditations on your past, it is important to enter a deep level of meditation by presenting your own experience to yourself in a vivid way, reflecting calmly about it and reliving it. The following exercises may perhaps be found valuable simply as reflections.

(a) In the evening

Look back at the day, recall what you have experienced and place it in the centre of your thoughts. Or else you may prefer to ask yourself: Was I active in doing or was I passive in a series of events? Or else re-enact the happenings of the day in God's presence and thank him, ask him to forgive you and give yourself up to him.

(b) At other times

Especially after certain events or experiences which seem to you to be particularly significant, on days of recollection, at the weekend or at the end of the year . . .

3. Forward-looking meditations

(a) In the morning.

Consider in advance the events and encounters that are likely to take place — these will and should be my own experience for today. Or think, for example: What is really important? What is going to be really significant in my life today? Or ask yourself in God's presence: What have you in store for me today? What is your will for me in my encounters with other people? What do you expect of me, what attitude, what words? What do you want me to do? Ask God these and other questions, look forward to the day ahead and prepare in advance what you hope to do and say as far as you are able.

(b) At other times

For example, before important discussions or interviews, before a special visit to a relative or friend or even to the theatre . . .

4. My present status in life

As someone who is trained for later life, as a married person, as a mother, as someone in a position of responsibility . . .

5. Others

Our lives are spent above all in relationships with others. We have to meditate about these relationships. All through our lives, we have the constant task of meditating about the other sex — thinking our way into the reality of man or woman in order to reach an understanding. We have to do the same with others who are younger or older than we are — to understand them by entering into their lives and trying to grasp the different reality that they are from within. This is a prerequisite for any happy and fruitful life lived together with others.

It is only when we come to observe the distinctive quality that characterizes other people that we shall ever begin to find true community with them. To allow this community to develop, we have then to go on to give this distinctive quality space to grow, let ourselves become quite open to it and fully accept it. In this way, our lives as individuals will become united with those of others and community will become a reality.

6. What is most original in yourself

In meditation, give space and freedom to what is quite peculiar to yourself and allow this to be expressed. Try to overcome all alienation. What is truly original in yourself? You should aim above all to come into contact with this. Find out, by a process of patient meditation, the affinity that exists between you and the people and things surrounding you. Discover what brings this originality that you possess to life and what will therefore enable you to become most fully yourself.

We should look for closer and deeper links with that originality — that origin from which we come and which keeps us alive. We should never accept a life led in the independence of limited individuality, but must above all seek the infinitely more satisfying life that is based on the ultimate and great reality of the mystery of our being. It is in communication with this great mystery that we should live, act and suffer.

PART II

SPECIAL SPHERES OF NATURAL MEDITATION

I SIMPLE ACTIONS

Regular, simple actions lend themselves easily to meditation. Such basic human actions are on the one hand part of our present experience and on the other always performed regularly. This makes them a very suitable subject for meditation.

1. I see — a text for guidance

At this moment I am seeing and experiencing everything. What do I in fact see? So much, down to the last detail . . . I am astonished how everything that I see can enter into my experience in this way! It is as though I were standing at a viewpoint and, through my eyes, the whole panorama were entering my being — forests, fields, hills and villages . .. . Yet it is only in my memory that I see all this.

I remember and reflect about all that I have ever seen. I think about all that has been given to me in this way, through seeing . . .

I try to imagine how I would have been had I been blind from birth . . . knowing only what came to me through feeling and hearing . . . no colours, no view of the countryside, no human face, nothing visible . . . Everything that has been given to me through my eyes, everything that I have seen . . .

Through my eyes I am constantly taking coloured photographs. I am like a camera making an endless film in colour . . . Everything that I have seen somehow remains within me . . . I am building up a great collection of visual memories. Without effort, I am able to call so much to mind — my own room, my parents' house where I was brought up, the streets that I knew then, the countryside where we spent our holidays, the faces of all the members of my family . . . so many pictures . . .works of art that I have contemplated . . . gifts that cannot be measured have been given to me through my power to see . . . I see all these people and things again and remain quietly resting in this act of seeing, this incomprehensible, yet very simple action . . . In it, I am conscious of a certain astonishment and have a premonition of the incomprehensible reality from which my present experience comes . . .

2. I hear — a text for guidance

What do I hear at this moment? Sounds? Steps? Voices? . . . Music, the words of a play, poetry . . . I am at a concert. In front of me I hear the sound of strings and wind instruments. Sound waves come towards me and a great edifice of rhythm and harmony is built up inside me — a work of art, a symphony . . .

While I hear the music, the dead composer's spirit as it were penetrates into the innermost recesses of my being. This experience is almost incomprehensible and I can only marvel at it . . .

I hear the voice of another person, addressing a group of people. Sounds rise up from within the speaker and form sentences . . . His words are invisible, but they reach me and enter me, so that his thoughts become mine . . .

I hear a word of love. The voice of my mother, of my husband or my wife . . . It sounds different from usual and I know that I am understood, accepted and loved . . .

I try to imagine what it is like to be deaf and to see only the movements of people's lips and hear nothing . . . People exchanging words, but I am excluded . . . I see another person who seems to be friendly towards me, but I cannot hear what he wants to say to me. He turns away from me . . . I see someone playing the violin, watch the movement of his bow and see his fingers on the strings, but no sound reaches me . . .

If I were deaf, all the music that I have ever received into my being — the songs I heard and sang as a child, my own singing and music making, the music I have heard so often on the radio and on records — would not have existed for me . . .

How much has entered me through my ability to hear! I remain quietly meditating about and remembering all that has reached my inner being through my ears.

3. I breathe — a text for guidance

I let my breath flow at will. It comes and goes of its own accord . . .
I observe the passage of air in my nostrils . . . In this way, I recognize, the air is made damp, warm and clean. I am conscious of the
air flowing past, behind and above the palate . . . of the air flowing
through the bronchial tubes into my lungs . . . I feel my diaphragm
expanding and contracting . . . I perceive my own breathing in and
out . . .

I know that the oxygen that I inhale goes from my lungs into my
blood. Their surface is as great as that of a tennis court. I follow the
flow of my blood with its new oxygen through all the parts of my
body — trunk, legs, feet, arms, hands and head . . . my whole body
is filled with blood . . .

This new oxygen in my body is used for combustion . . . the
effect of breathing can be felt wherever it is warm. I feel the warmth
that is carried by my breath . . .

I know how dependent I am on the air that surrounds me and on
my breathing it. I breathe out and try not to breathe in for as long
as I can manage. But I have to breathe in eventually. I depend on the
air around me . . . I have to receive the gift of air constantly. My life
depends entirely on being given air all the time . . .

Where does this gift of air come from? For several hundred
million years the air has been formed by the plants of the earth and
especially by the trees. There have been hundreds of millions of years
of preparation for me to be able to breathe and live here . . . Yet the
layer of air around the earth's surface is as thin as a wrapping paper
around an orange. And without it, I could not live . . .

I breathe and experience breathing as a gift . . . everything happens
as it were of its own accord. Everything is there, ready for me and
given to me . . . What lies behind this gift? What benevolent, refreshing, generous power? It is good to breathe and at the same time to
experience the ultimate mystery of my being and of all being . . .

4. I walk — a testimony

In this testimony, there is a transition from a natural meditation

*about walking to a meditation about faith in God. Use this testi-
mony, provided by someone else, as a basis for your own meditation.*

I was walking along a lonely road. I had no intention apart
from that of simply walking. Gradually I became aware of the
incomprehensible fact that I was walking. I did not know how I
was able to preserve my balance or how my legs were able to move
as they did. I did not know how I was able to walk. All that I knew
was that I was able. I had an intense experience simply of my own
walking.

Then I thought: Where are you in fact going? The answer came:
to the forest. But immediately I thought: What is your real goal?
And I thought of God and his kingdom and the fulfilment of man
and of all creation. I was walking towards that.

How, then, am I walking? I am walking towards God through
every day in which I carry out his will and by means of every good
action that I perform in accordance with his will. Every step that I
take in this spirit is a step towards God. It is good that I should
walk in this way.

I began to experience every step that I took as a step towards
God. Nearer and nearer to God. My experience became more and
more intense until it was almost overwhelming. I knew that he
was calling me, drawing me forward and accompanying me on the
way. I went on walking and this intense experience remained with
me.

5. I shall sleep — leading to a forward-looking meditation

It is late. It is time for me to sleep. I review in my mind what I
shall do: clear up, go to the bathroom, get the bed ready, get undres-
sed and lie down in bed . . .

I shall give up all conscious possession of myself, let myself go
completely and surrender myself to the power of sleep. I shall
entrust myself entirely to sleep . . .

How deeply will it penetrate into my inner being, this entrusting
myself to sleep? Will it only go as far as the bed on which I lie?
Will it only go a little further than that — as far as the blankets
that keep me warm? Or will it go much further — into inner depth of

my being, so that the whole of my conscious life is embraced in it? Or will it perhaps go to the ultimate depth, to the one who holds me in the palm of his hand . . . to the one in whom I find security?

I lie down. I am held by him. I am secure. In this way I can express something of my security in God and my ultimate trust in him . . .

Other models for this type of meditation are, for example:

I am working; I have breakfast; I am sitting down; I am reading; I am silent. Any one of these simple actions can lead to the kind of meditation and inner experience outlined above. I must find the one that is most suitable for me.

II SIMPLE THINGS

All things have something to say to us. We should therefore let them express themselves when we meditate. To do this we must, of course, remain silent and receptive. Things can in this way become symbols for us.

1. Beside a stream — leading to meditation

Sit down beside a stream or river. When you are completely peaceful and recollected, allow yourself to be open to what the water flowing past you has to say.

2. Water — leading to meditation

It is better to choose, if possible, a place where you can see natural water — the bank of a lake, on the coast or by a spring. If not, have a large bowl of clear water in front of you. Your meditation will be more successful if you drink some of the water first, put your hands and face into it and, in the case of a lake or the sea, swim in it . . .

In the course of this meditation, look steadily at the water and think of the various ways in which you have encountered water in your life: How have you seen it? What has it done to you? What have you done with it? Has it made you happy in any way? Threatened you? What has it given to you? How does it serve you? What is its use in your life? . . . Let all these memories and experiences of water in your life be made present by the water that you are now contemplating in front of you. Remain quietly in the presence of those experiences . . . If astonishment or thankfulness rise up inside you during this meditation, let these feelings remain too . . .

This meditation can be repeated as often as you like. You may also wish to use certain passages from the Bible or short texts such as being 'born of water and the Spirit' (John 3. 5; see also John 4. 7; 7. 37-39).

3. A stream in winter — a testimony

This testimony shows the way in which a meditation about a natural object can develop. I include it here less as an example to be followed — it is obvious that many readers will not easily be able to contemplate a real stream in winter — than as an indication as to how such a meditation about a natural object can be taken to the deeper level of meditation about a symbol and thus affect one's whole attitude to life.

I was walking along the narrow road leading into the valley. It followed a little stream, which was only about four yards wide and which sometimes flowed very close to the road and at other times a little further away. I stopped in order to see more closely what was happening. What a varied image the stream presented! I had a good view of a large part of it from where I was standing . . . and how much I could see taking place!

The waves — and how many there were — were dancing and springing before my eyes. There was constant movement. The water flowed and foamed, beating against the banks and against a counter-current, rising up and sinking down. It was one great, yet constantly interrupted movement towards a distant, unseen objective. And there was unceasing noise — gurgling, lapping, rushing and murmuring. What I was watching was really a single process, although it seemed to be divided, and the stream was, in a sense, fulfilling its essential task, doing what it had to do, in accordance with its essential nature, . . .

Then I understood that a great deal more than this was taking place before my eyes. Parts of the stream were frozen over — large areas of ice had survived from the colder weather and had become prettily covered by the energetic flow of the water above them. Yet I could see water flowing beneath these flat surfaces of ice, and it was full of bubbles, dancing and vibrating. Some of these flat sheets of ice, much nearer the surface of the stream, were covered with trickles of water, and a few joined others to form smaller streams within the one great stream.

At one point, I could see the current striking a large stone near the surface. Part of this stone was standing above the water level, still covered with snow from the fall of a few days before — snow pitted with little holes made by spray from the water of the stream. In another place in the stream, ice had piled up into a rough dam. The water, beating against this barrier and unable to break through it, was turning aside, running in almost the opposite direction to the current for a little way and eventually flowing into the main stream, where it continued downwards into the valley.

So much was happening! So much movement in the water — running, dancing, leaping, striking, pushing, letting go, being carried along. And so much noise — gurgling, rushing, hissing, roaring, murmuring. All this made up part of the form of pure, clear water in constant, never-ending change. And there were the blocks and sheets of ice, the snow and the spray — all different forms of the one water . . . All these different processes could be expressed in the one simple phrase 'perfect obedience'. The water's obedience to its own essential being . . . One single process was taking place in front of me, within the many different forms and shapes — a perfect and total obedience. Apart from this obedience, nothing was happening. Obedience was being expressed in many different ways. This obviously led me to reflect about obedience in my own life . . .

At the same time, however, I was reminded of another law that was expressed in what was taking place before my eyes in the stream — nature's response to the situation. This was clearly what the stream was doing and, what was more, it was doing it in a perfect way. Nowhere was the situation overlooked. Everything that I could see was a perfect response to the situation. The stream was responding everywhere to the valley, to the bed of the stream, to the stones, the temperature and the conditions imposed by the weather. All that I could see in front of me in all its many forms, became in this way a rich and wonderful symbol of my own life and of the task that I had to fulfil . . . Indeed, it was a symbol of human life as such and of the task that we all have to carry out in response to the situation, to everything that we encounter in our lives and to every gift that we receive . . .

I stood still for a long time, gazing at the stream in winter. I became more and more conscious of the thought of pure obedience to the essential task that confronts us in life. And as I became more and more aware of this, I began to understand more and more deeply that every good action that we perform is determined by those two factors — perfect obedience to our inner being and perfect response to the situation in which we find ourselves.

Finally, I knew that the great driving force of all human life was love and that this was expressed in perfect obedience to God's will for us and in service of our fellow men. Even now, long afterwards, I can still call the stream in winter to mind and am conscious of its symbolic value, which speaks to me of perfect obedience motivated by love.

4. The ground — a testimony

I went past a recently ploughed field. This led me to meditate about the ground — about earth. I sat down and picked up a handful of earth, smelled it, pressed it down between my palms and crumbled it. In this way, I came into close contact with it. I let it fall between my fingers. I thought of the words — earthy, fresh, fruitful, fertile . . .

Then I looked down at the ground and thought how wonderful it was. I thought of the many organisms living in a single lump of earth and making it possible for plants to grow in the soil. Then I thought of everything produced from the ground. The words of

Scripture, in the story of creation, occurred to me: 'Let the earth put forth . . .' And I remembered how we all depend on the earth for our lives. How I depend on it, 'mother earth'.

My next thought was that we all return to the earth and that I shall one day rest in it. Adam, the man whom God fashioned out of dust from the ground. I am Adam and I felt at one with him. Finally, I thought of the words that might perhaps be on my grave: Rest in God.

5. Bread — leading to meditation

Place a loaf of bread in front of you on the table, be quite peaceful and let the bread have its effect on you. Let what it has to say penetrate completely into you. If you find this difficult, ask about its origin and how it came to be what it is now. Then go on to meditate about how dependent you are on bread for nourishment. The next stage is to think about its value as a symbol. Remain at each stage for as long as it is profitable. You can also allow the words 'bread of life' to be heard inside you.

6. The key — a text leading to several days' meditation

Cover the table with a cloth of a neutral colour and place the key to your house or your own room on it in front of you.

What do I see? A piece of metal with a short round shaft, at one end of which is a ring, at the other the flat, toothed part that is inserted into the lock. That is all that is seen of this simple thing in front of me.

Now let this thing have its effect on you. Is it not meaningless as it is? It only has a meaning when it is inserted into a lock. And, what is more, when it is inserted into a lock in a door or lid . . . Even more, the door must close a room or the lid must close a box . . . even more, this piece of metal must be used as a key by a person . . . What, then, is quite striking is that this piece of metal that is in front of me now only becomes a key, in other words, it only becomes what it is, when it has this function and this relationship

The world that is comprised in this key can open even more. It can disclose all the experiences that I have had with this key or with other keys . . . The door to my own room — locked from inside or from outside . . . I myself, sitting in my room . . . The person outside . . . Security, being undisturbed, being imprisoned, being free, being shut out and excluded . . . I think of all these experiences and situations brought about in my life and in the lives of others by this key, by other keys . . . The key to my desk . . . The car key . . . All that they can mean to a man, to a woman . . .

The same can also take place in the sphere of our own lives. Something can be revealed to someone — a landscape, a work of art, a text, a word or a conversation that opens a world of meaning . . . Where, when did you experience that? . . . A young person closed in on himself becomes open . . . He is set free . . . A closed expression on someone's face, an open expression . . . Closing oneself to an experience . . . Opening oneself to someone . . . Have I ever opened anything to anyone? . . . For whom am I the key? Who has ever disclosed anything to me? Who has been a key for me? The key to a problem . . . A great deal will be opened to anyone who tries honestly to answer these and similar questions.

Opening oneself to God. It is finally obvious to me that, if we are to open ourselves to God, he must make us open: 'The Lord opened Lydia's heart to give heed to what was said by Paul' (Acts 16. 14). What, then, is there in me that is closed to God? . . . Are there any experiences that have occurred in the depth of my being that have been the cause of God's having opened himself to me? . . . Or has he recently opened himself in any way to me? . . . The Church used to sing of Christ: 'O Key of David, . . . who openest and no man shutteth, who shuttest and no man openeth'. To what extent have I been open to God's opening of himself to me in Christ?

The turning, spiral movement of the key continues higher and higher and wider and wider, seeking to open more and more and to disclose deeper and deeper meanings. At the same time, all this height, width and depth return in the spiral and are contained mysteriously within the key.

7. Fruit

This material should enable you to prepare a number of meditations of your own. It is a good idea to have some fruit and a sheet of paper in front of you. Failing this, you can use a picture showing fruit. There are two stages in the meditative process that follows — the preparation and the meditation proper. You can either use the whole of the text in the preparation and then go on to interiorize the experience in meditation or else simply deepen your inner experience of one or two parts of the preparatory text that you have chosen.

Fruit that I have eaten . . . I call to mind and think about all the different kinds of fruit, see them in my mind's eye and perhaps note them down.

The world of fruit . . . their effect on us . . . when we see various fruit . . . when we taste them . . . some ideas about fruit and their effect on us may be worth noting down . . .

Look up Psalm 65, verses 10—14. Read the text and meditate it.

Find other texts in the Bible that deal with man's bearing fruit. Some examples are Mt. 3. 8-10; 7. 16-17; 13. 23; Jn. 15. 1-5. Then ask yourself: what fruit am I bearing? In what ways can I take this idea of bearing fruit to a deeper level in my own life?

Write down the text of John 15. 3: 'You are already made clean by the word which I have spoken to you'. You may find it profitable to meditate how we are impelled to bear fruit by the power of Christ. Deepen this meditation if you find it useful.

Look up Gal. 5. 22-23 and meditate about the fruit of the Spirit. If you continue with this meditation, you may reach the point where you become conscious of their presence in you and their effect on your behaviour.

The day of the harvest. What references to this can be found in the New Testament? Ask yourself: What kind of fruit will I bear? What fruit will my whole generation bear?

You can close this whole preparation with a reflection about John 15. 16.

There should be sufficient material here for a week's preparation. You can then go on to the meditation proper.

8. The bowl – leading to your own meditation

Place a bowl on the table in front of you. You should choose one with as simple and as beautiful a shape as possible and the table should otherwise be empty. Let the bowl have its effect on you, first as a whole and then using such questions as: What is it doing to me? What does its shape say to me? What is its essence? What does it stand for as a symbol? You can then go further, taking your eyes from the bowl itself, closing them and contemplating the essence of the bowl interiorly . . .

9. The electric current – a stimulus

I have to clean the house today with the vacuum cleaner. I find that it is often possible to become quiet and recollected while I am doing this work, with its regular movement and the humming of the motor. It might perhaps be worth while to meditate about the electric current . . .

Its effect is felt through my hands. I am conscious of the gentle vibration of the vacuum cleaner. I can hear the noise of the motor . . . I can see its effect . . . The vacuum cleaner is driven by the electric current . . .

I look at the cleaner, then at the lead . . . then at the plug . . . I think of the mysterious force called 'voltage'. How does it come about?

The house is connected with the local power station . . . This makes me think of the machinery, the people employed in the service, the many effects of electricity . . .

What would happen if the electricity were cut off or were to fail? It is not difficult to imagine. I think about this and its effects. . .

My body too is full of currents and how little I understand of it . . . How mysterious electricity is . . . a great gift, given to us for us to use in our homes . . . Our whole way of life depends on the invisible presence of electricity, which brings people together and moves machinery . . . A meditation in depth about this mystery ought to yield results . . . Perhaps the electric current is also a symbol? . . .

I will begin now. I only hope the telephone does not ring.

10. Other simple things

A tree, flowers, rain, the bridge, the table, a book, the telephone, my right hand, words and language . . . The prerequisite for any meditation about these and similar things is that they should be perceived as a totality. That should be our point of departure, from which to begin to meditate about them and move on, by way of the basic excercises, to the inner depth where they can have an effect on us and say something to us.

III WORKS OF ART

1. Pictures

If you have a picture that seems to you to be suitable for meditation, sit in front of it and proceed in the following way. First, let your gaze wander all over the picture, slowly so that you are able to perceive everything, down to the last detail (This is total perception.) Then ask yourself a number of questions. For example, who was the painter? To what period did he belong? What is the subject of the picture? What is the artist trying to say to me? Now go more deeply into the artistic form of the painting – its structure, the way in which the brush has been used, the individual shapes and the details within the picture as a whole. In this way, you will come closer to an understanding of the artist's intention. Finally, look at the painting as a whole and consider what it has to tell you.

Listen to the painter through his work and let the depth of his experience, as expressed in the picture, enter into the depth of your own being. To allow this to happen, you will probably want sometimes to continue to contemplate the painting peacefully and at other times — especially when the artist's work has fully penetrated to your innermost being — to close your eyes.

If you are not sure which picture or pictures to choose for meditation of this kind, you should consult someone who is experienced in this selection.

2. Vocal music with texts

Several works are particularly suitable for this kind of meditation — Haydn's 'Creation', Handel's 'Messiah' and the Passions by Bach or Heinrich Schutz. Almost all oratorios lend themselves easily to meditation. It is well worth reading the text quietly beforehand and allowing it to penetrate as deeply as possible. It is quite permissible to keep the text in front of you while you listen, or to put it aside if you prefer. While you are listening, let the words and the music sink into your innermost being. The text will be interpreted and deepened by the music that originally resulted from the composer's meditation and in which we take part in our meditation. It is important to begin silently, peacefully and in a state of recollection, so that you are able to receive the words and the music meditatively.

IV   OUR FELLOW MEN

Wait until you have found both nearness and distance. You should be near enough to have a positive encounter with your neighbour and at the same time you should be distant. You will know that you have achieved this distance when you are conscious that all movement of your emotions has ceased and you are peaceful and recollected. When you have reached this point, you will be able to ask yourself an almost objective question which nonetheless reflects love and deep concern for your fellow man or woman: What is he or she really like?

1. My father − text leading to meditation or for guidance

First go through the following model reading all the questions. Other questions may suggest themselves to you. Then free your mind of them. Carry out a preparatory exercise to become peaceful and recollected and from this to move into an attitude of total perceptivity. Alternatively, try asking yourself one question after the other and reflecting about them at length until you begin to experience in depth.

What is my experience of my father? What is he like in his free time? What is he like professionally, in his work, with his colleagues? What is his personal history? What does it mean to him to be married to this woman, my mother? What is his attitude towards me? What is his relationship with me, my brothers and sisters?

He is a man. Does that mean anything to me? . . . As a human being, he inevitably has certain limitations and shortcomings. What are his positive characteristics? . . . How should I really look at him in order to see him as he is?

Pause for as long as you can, meditating about the insights that you have gained from this reflection about your father. You may, with patience, learn how to live on better terms with him.

2. A forward-looking meditation about one's husband or wife − leading to meditation

The following text is principally for husbands and wives, but it can also be used, suitably adapted, by engaged couples, or even by those who have just come to love each other.

Before your next date or your next meeting, before you go out together, before you go home to your partner or before any deep encounter in marriage, use the fundamental exercise to become completely peaceful, composed and recollected. Then contemplate

your partner in your innermost being and let the focal point of
your love move away from yourself and be concentrated on the
other. Turn, in other words, from 'I' to 'You'. Let your love be you-
related rather than I-centred. With patience and by this process
of empathetic meditation, you will gradually come to understand
your partner and your relationship with him or her better. A number
of questions will arise and you should try to answer them honestly.
    What is he really like? How does he feel? What are his feelings?
What are his expectations? What, in his recent experience, was
successful? What was unsuccessful? What was not good in my
attitude towards him? In any encounter with me, how is *his* life
improved, how does *he* move towards greater maturity, how is *he*
fulfilled? What is he really like when he is positively orientated?
What can I do, in my attitude towards him, to ensure that he is positively orientated and that he will benefit from encounter with me?
How can I make sure that his life will become deeper and that he
will be enriched by our relationship? That we shall go forward
together, become more alert to each other and better for each
other? That we shall learn to understand each other more deeply
and to see each other more completely? That everything in my
body and spirit, all that is peculiar to me and to my deepest and
essential self, all that most truthfully reflects not simply an ideal
picture of myself, but what I really am penetrates into his innermost
being? What should I do to enable everything that most completely
expresses what I am to reach him?
    This meditation should lead to a selflessness and to the presence
of your partner with you in a very complete, though spiritual
sense.

3. You are invited out – a model

*The following model should not be used as an exercise in abstract
meditation, but rather as something that is carried out in a spirit
of recollection within the particular situation in which you find
yourself.*

    You have been invited out by a young married couple to spend
the evening with them. You can, of course, go to see them, share

their meal and talk about trivialities. On the other hand, you can approach the whole matter quite differently. While you are still at home changing for the evening, begin to think about the couple and ask yourself questions such as the following about them.

Who are they? What do I know about them? How did our last conversation go off? What really interests them? What can I tell them that will concern them? To what end should I direct the talk? What do they like talking about? How can I arrange it so that they will express their real interests, while I remain silent and listen? What sort of questions should I ask them so that they give valid answers and the whole conversation is worth while? What particular aspects of their outlook can I remember? In what ways do we complement each other?

Questions like these should be passing through your mind while you are preparing for the visit. They will make you alert to the encounter and its needs.

You can also meditate in advance about their marriage itself. You may perhaps, on a previous occasion, have noticed some of the ways in which they annoy each other or stimulate each other, some of the causes of harmony or disharmony between them. Think about their home. What struck you about it? In what ways did it indicate that they were simple people or pretentious people, helpless or artistic? Or think about the way in which the young wife has prepared for your visit. She wants above all to be a good hostess. She has set the table, put flowers in a vase and been busy getting the meal ready in the kitchen. She must have given a good deal of thought to the appearance of the table and everything on it. She has tried to make her home warm, pleasant and hospitable for you . . .

You leave your own house and every step that you take brings you nearer to them, not simply to their house, but to their home, themselves and their marriage. Going through the streets should be part of a meditative process, an action in which you draw inwardly nearer to them. If this process is complete on your arrival, you will be entirely alert to them and their needs, completely ready and recollected. An evening about which you have meditated in advance in this way ought to be a very good and successful one.

There are, of course, many other human experiences about which forward-looking meditations can be made — a letter that has to be written, what to say after a misunderstanding, an encounter with someone you love, a negotiation in which you have to take part, a visit to the theatre. This meditation in advance is often, of course, something that we tend to do automatically, but it is worth thinking carefully about how to do it. If we practise it at a deep level, we shall become more and more clear to ourselves and more and more fully present for our fellow men.

4. Other people

It is clearly very important to meditate about all the other people with whom we have a great deal to do and with whom we are, in one way or another, closely connected. We should always be concerned to understand them from within and to penetrate into the mystery of their being from the point of departure of their words and actions. In this way, we should be able to discover them lovingly and caringly and to do full justice to them as different beings. It is also worth while to reflect about the more negative aspects of their being, but this should not form part of the meditation itself, which is only concerned with their positive aspects and has an exclusively positive aim.

V   MEDITATING IN OUR BODILY EXPRESSION

Meditation is in no sense purely spiritual. It is a fully human process, in which our body is included. We can include our body in the meditative process in four different ways — by the position of our body in meditation, by our attitude of inner physical and spiritual repose at depth, in other words, our state of hara, by our breathing and by our words.

It is, however, also possible to begin meditating in the body itself, in which case the content of your meditation will be your physical, bodily state. Your interior experience will be borne by and will in turn inspire your body. You will find that this will take place more easily if you patiently learn to perceive the state of your body, either while you are motionless or while you are making very slow, free movements. A few examples of this type of meditation are given below.

1. I sit in one of the positions for meditation and perceive its effect on me. I am conscious that it brings peace.

2. I perceive my breathing. I am conscious of it as an act of receiving, as an activity that is taking place in me, through me and even without me . . . What has it to say to me?

3. I sit in one of the positions for meditation and after a little while place my hands on my knees, palms uppermost . . . What do I feel in my palms? What do my hands express in this position? What do they tell me? What depths of meaning do I receive through them?

4. I am sitting in a position for meditation and am in an attitude of hara. My hands are resting, palms downward, on my knees. Now I let a petition form itself deep within me and rise up as a longing to receive. I let it pass slowly into my right arm, move up into my hand and express itself there. When this movement has ceased and I am completely at rest again, I let the same petition pass into my left arm and hand . . . In this way, it takes about two minutes for my hands to free themselves and be raised up, turned and opened, first the right hand, then the left, until the whole gesture and, in it, my whole body — and indeed my whole being — has become an expression of petition and longing, expecting and receiving.

We should not perform movements of this kind ourselves; we should rather receive them from within ourselves. They should, as it were, come of their own accord like new leaves in spring, as a bodily expression of processes that are already present and taking place within us.

5. I sit and am filled with a deep desire to express humility, reverence, homage and adoration with my whole being. I go through the 'I am here' exercise (see pp. 20-22) and this enables me to have the correct spiritual attitude, so that I can wait patiently and see what begins to take place within me. My right arm may perhaps move into a gesture of submission and worship . . . I let my whole

body follow this movement and express itself in adoration . . . My
shoes are off and I slowly kneel . . . I sit on my heels and wait . . .
Slowly I bend forward . . . My arms are stretched out . . . My forehead is resting on the ground . . . This bodily expression has come
entirely from within me . . . I let it return to within me and have
its effect on my innermost being . . . I wait patiently, meditate
about this deep interior experience and remain in an attitude of
meditation . . .

6.   I am an anemone opening, blooming and wilting. Imagine
that you are beside a stream with other anemones closed or partly
closed around you. It is in March, early in the morning. Sit on your
heels, kneeling, with your forehead touching the ground.

I am this windflower. I experience a powerful urge to grow
and to open up in full bloom. (Do not simply 'imitate' this process
of blooming.) I wait until this urge comes to the point of movement.
Slowly my back begins to lift itself up . . . My forehead leaves the
ground . . . The upper part of my body begins to straighten up . . .
My arms are still hanging loosely . . . As I straighten up my hands
continue to brush to and fro over the ground . . . My face is as it
is when I am asleep . . . Very slowly the process is completed and the
upper part of my body is straight. But my arms are still limp . . .
Gently I put one foot in front of me and put the toes of my other
foot, which is still underneath me, on to the ground. Very slowly
I stand up. Just as slowly, my arms begin to raise themselves, my
hands remaining limp . . . I am standing with my feet together and
my arms stretched upwards. My fingers are wide apart. My face is
upturned to receive the warm rays of the sun . . . The whole process
lasts between three and five minutes.

Now I begin to wilt. First my face . . . Then my hands hang down
limply . . . My arms slowly fall . . . My whole body wilts slowly,
becoming looser and limper until I am once again in the position
where I began.

You must experience the whole process within yourself and let
it happen of its own accord as a bodily expression of an inner
experience, the bodily expression having its effect in turn on your
inner experience. Never simply 'imitate' the movement of the windflower — you must be one!

7.   Other variations on the same theme of bodily expression are

slavery and liberation, despair and the approach of love; I have found something. In all these examples, observe the basic rules: let the movement of your body come from your inner experience and move slowly and with the whole of your self, body and spirit. Let yourself flow into the movement.

Try standing with legs apart. But feel and experience this standing. Wait until a movement takes place. Give way to this movement. It may be a movement of *mowing*, one of *sowing* or one of *giving*. There may be movements without any clearly defined theme: larger, all-embracing movements; playful gestures without any aim; movements expressing you and your life.

Put on a record with a simple musical theme, or chamber music if you like. Listen to it several times. Wait until the music turns into dancing within you. Then give way to the movements. For all these physical excercises it is best to wear very light, freely-fitting clothes. You should find yourself through bodily expression, and come to perfect freedom, inner joy, and peace.

VI   EXISTENTIAL MEDITATIONS

When you begin to meditate existentially, you should ask yourself such questions as: What am I really like as a person? What is my existence? How ought I, in that existence, to behave? What should my attitude be? How should I realize my existence? You should examine various aspects of your existence and try to understand them in depth. As you become more mature and gain in consciousness of your own existence through meditation, you will be able to accept these aspects of yourself more and more as realities.

The procedure should begin with a meditation of short statements such as those given later in this chapter. It is easier to carry it out if you look into your own experience for events, occasions and realities that have been existentially meaningful. Recall these significant existential realities, reflect about them and discover in this way what they really mean. You can, as it were, circle round the statement that you are considering in a constantly widening spiral movement.

As soon as you feel yourself to be deeply affected by the total reality that you have discovered, go back to the simple statement in the text for guidance with the understanding that you have gained of yourself and your own existence. Remain at that point – it is the point at which your meditation proper begins. Pause, look at the existential reality that you have grasped in this process and let it penetrate to your innermost being. If you carry out this exercise properly, your knowledge of your own existence will become more mature, deeper and fuller and you will be moving towards a more complete humanity.

It is also possible to discover a very special kind of experience in practising this type of existential meditation. In coming to understand our own existence in this way, we become aware of another reality, one which is not ourselves and is indeed different from ourselves. This ultimate reality makes itself felt in our existence – in our questions about the meaning of life, our expectations of life and our sense of responsibility. If you reach this deep level in meditation, you should open yourself fully to the experience and remain within it. In the exercises that follow it is important to go beyond the mere reflection and to reach this point in meditation. It is only when you are fully at peace in a state of silent receptivity that this ultimate reality will have its effect on you and disclose its inner meaning to you.

1. I am – a text for guidance

I place this text in front of me on the table, having cleared away all other reading material. I now begin to prepare myself with the aim of acquiring an attitude of complete peace, uninhibited presence and total depth. Only then do I begin to read the following text.

(a)　　I find myself here at this moment. I am here in this room, at this time, in this chair, sitting in front of this table. That is an indisputable fact – I am here. I am. I simply find myself here. Yet how remarkable it is! I can see myself. I can touch myself. I find myself here as this particular person, with this name, with this – my – history, with this body and with this sex. I find myself

here, seeing, hearing, breathing . . . How strange it is that I should be here. I am conscious of the fact and of myself . . . It is a simple fact — I am. I cannot escape from myself and my own existence. Even if I were to kill myself, I would not be able to release myself from that existence — I would probably simply change the mode of my existence. It is a strange, yet undeniable and inescapable fact — I find myself here. Where does this great strength come from, this power that makes my existence here so lasting? So that I know that I am here constantly?

I am sitting here in this existence, my existence. I am sitting here now and I go on sitting . . . as if I were in a train that I cannot leave. No one has ever asked me if I really wanted to begin to live as this particular person and to carry on living this life. My existence began without my having been asked and now I simply find myself here. Who, then, is in control of me in this way? Who decided for me? I could be very indignant about it! On the other hand, how could I have been asked before I was there? That would have been impossible. That I am simply here is very mysterious. In any case, I simply have to accept the fact that my existence is controlled, as it were, externally. But what lies behind it?

Or is it not simply a question of nature that I am here? There are, of course, biological reasons for my existence. My father and mother got to know each other . . . This thread can be traced back to the first living organisms on earth . . . But is this sufficient as an explanation? Is there a purpose in my existence? An aim? Like a finished car, straight from the assembly line? There are many different causes, but the car was wanted and it had a purpose. So it is there. And it is this particular car. What about me? There must have been so many causes contributing to make me what I am. I too was wanted. My existence has a purpose. But who wants me? As I am? Who has wanted and accepted me so completely that I am here, without doing anything, without any effort at all on my part? For I must have been wanted and accepted completely by someone . . .

(b)   I am here — but not of my own accord. My existence cannot be without aim or purpose. It did not simply come about with no aim or reason. What, then, is the ultimate goal of my being?

I am on the way, but what is my destination? I am sitting in a train and cannot leave it, but where is that train going? What is the meaning of my existence? What is the end of this journey? I am able to do many things — I can see, feel, walk . . . But all these activities must have a meaning. What is meaningful in my life? I can do various kinds of work. I can carry out a profession . . . I can help other people . . . be present for them, available to them . . . These activities give meaning to my existence . . .

But these are just shreds of meaning, isolated fragments. What, then, is the whole meaning of my existence? Why am I, as a whole, here? And what is the whole reality for which I am here? Is it the whole of mankind? But this, surely, is a reality which I can never reach. I can only reach individuals. Are individual people, then, my destination? I experience myself as a whole being. My existence has many different aspects and contains many possibilities, but I am nonetheless a single whole. Does this whole, which I am, therefore have these separate individuals as its aim? I cannot believe that my whole existence is directed towards these individuals whom I help and for whom I work, because only part of what I am, not my whole being, is at their service and only with a few actions that I perform . . . They only perceive a little of me . . . They are only able to make use of a small part of me . . . And I frequently only annoy them . . . They cannot be my whole aim in life and I cannot be directed exclusively towards them. What, then, is the meaning of my existence as a whole? Where am I going, I who find myself here, I who am? . . .

I am aware that I am constantly looking for and finding shreds and fragments of meaning, but that I can never find the whole meaning of my existence here. The ultimate goal of my existence, the ultimate reality of my being, everything that goes to form the ultimate meaning of my life here — this does not consist of shreds or fragments. It is a whole. This totality of being that I am emerges in the fragmentary glimpses I and others have of me. Behind, beyond and beneath all the partial meaning there is a depth of meaning, a mysterious totality in which everything comes together . . .

It is this wholeness to which my being is moving. This is what I am constantly seeking, consciously or unconsciously, with my whole being. This lies behind all the many partial and individual aims which are always attracting me, which to some extent fulfil me and which so soon disappoint me or else pass by, are lost, and leave me seeking some other aim . . .

I know now that the ultimate goal of my existence is not to be found in many different, new aims. An infinite number of fragments of meaning cannot really be the ultimate meaning of the whole of my existence. These are all ultimately unable to fulfil me. I cannot go on seeking horizontally. I have to look into the depths . . . I must look deeper . . . Beyond all the meaning that I find in individual people or separate realities in my existence there is a single, deeper meaning, the ultimate mystery in which all this partial meaning comes together . . . All the separate fragments of meaning come from that ultimate meaning, the mystery towards which my whole existence is directed. My existence is on the way towards that mystery. When I have reached it all meaninglessness will disappear from my life and I shall find fulfilment, peace and salvation.

2. I have received many gifts — leading to meditation

A few ideas are given below. They can serve as points of departure. You can make your own selection and develop the meditation in your own way.

(a) I see. I experience my own seeing. It works so easily. Different realities are now and all the time entering me — things, scenes, people . . . All this I experience. It all takes place without any effort on my part. It is given to me . . . I experience the gift of sight and remain quietly in it . . . I am blessed with this wonderful gift, which I have through no merit of my own . . . Many people cannot see . . . I can see everything that comes into me, everything that has ever entered me . . . I am not isolated from the world outside me . . . I have contact, through my seeing, with the world . . .

(b) In the same way I experience the gifts that I have received — hearing . . . breathing . . . walking . . .

(c) I meditate about my body and the physical and mental skills

that I have — that have been given to me . . . my eyes . . . my ears
. . . my nose . . . my mouth . . . my hands, feet . . . my power to
think, to make decisions, to desire, to persist in a task, to remember
. . . I remain as long as possible meditating about these realities and
experiencing them as intensely as possible as gifts. They are not
mine — they are given to me . . .

(d)   I experience myself as a whole, a single unity that has been
given to myself . . .

(e)   I look out at the world . . . at nature . . . at the garden . . .
at fruit set out for sale . . . at a forest . . . I experience all these as
gifts.

(f)   I recognize individual things that belong to me, my possessions, as gifts . . .

(g)   I experience all the people who know and love me as gifts . . .

3. I am designed — leading to meditation

The easiest way for me to understand myself as a whole being is
to think of myself as designed as a man or a woman. All that I can
do is to accept this design, slip into it and become fully and truly
a man or a woman . . . If I do not accept this design, I shall become
misformed, physically or mentally ill. How remarkable it is that I
have been designed as a man, as a woman . . .

I think of other aspects of my being that show how I am designed — I am designed to see, to walk, to make and fashion things,
to live together with others . . . None of this belongs to me . . . It
is strange to think that I have been designed . . . It can be experienced in many different individual ways . . . Meditating about
myself as having been designed and about the different ways in
which this design shows itself, I come to the ultimate depth of the
mystery of my being . . .

4. I am confronted with other forms and meaningful structures
– leading to meditation

I look for and consider a number of examples taken from the world
of plants and animals, from the realm of inorganic matter and from
that of molecules and atoms. Man is part of that world . . . I contemplate the way in which these organisms are fashioned . . . I see
them as they are . . .

As they are, they can be seen. They can also become transparent,
so that their deeper reality becomes clear . . . Like a painting, which
is transparent to the artist who painted it. What power fashioned
them? Of what power do I become conscious as I look at them?

5. I live in a constant state of obedience – leading to meditation

I cannot even hammer a nail into a piece of wood without obeying
all the laws involved in the process. All people – manual workers,
technicians, mathematicians and artists, for example – have to
obey certain laws. If they do not submit to these laws, the cupboard
door will jam, the aircraft propeller will not turn, the account will
be wrong and the picture will be incomprehensible. Everyone has
to obey laws – we all have to eat, use our eyes and ears, move . . .

I try to understand this state of total obedience in which I
live . . . I look for certain clear signs of it . . . individual examples of
this obedience . . . I let myself be affected as deeply as possible by
this existential reality – that I am absolutely dependent on what is
present in my environment and that I have to be obedient to its
laws – and recognize that I can only be truly free in obedience.
I meditate at a deep level about this mystery.

6. I live together with others – a text for guidance lasting
several days

We are concerned, in the exercise that follows, with an existential
reality that is almost too great to be seen as a whole. The meditation proper should be preceded by a preparatory activity in which

your powers of perception and understanding are sharpened. In using the text, you should seize on those points that are important for you and develop them at depth.

(a)   I live among other people. This may provide sufficient basis for an act of total perception . . .

(b)   I live from and through other people. My existence here has come to me from and through others. It has been given to me. It comes from my parents . . . from my ancestors . . .

Throughout my life I am always dependent on the services provided by other people. My home, the clothes I wear, what I eat . . . They all come from and through others . . .

What I know — how much of it comes from and through other people . . .

My whole personality, all that has gone to form me, depends on the fact that I am recognized and accepted by other people, counselled and helped by them and also criticized and opposed by them . . .

I inwardly contemplate my personality as a whole . . . So much of what appears to be essentially my own has come from others . . . Their lives have penetrated into mine . . . I also meditate about how other people continue to influence my life in so many ways . . . By their attitude towards me and their relationships with me they create an environment which may further or impede the progress of my life . . .

(c)   I live for others. My life is also directed towards other people . . . I fulfil myself by living for others . . . Do others live through me? I do not live like a tree, which grows from its own centre . . . My life is more like a bridge, reaching out towards others and enabling them to reach me . . . Who are those other people? . . . I try to understand what this living for others means in my life and for my personality.

(d)   I live in others. I am in others — the other people who think about me, accept me, love me and help to sustain me. I exist in those who would be deprived if I were to die . . .

I contemplate this reality . . . My existence is not limited by my own body . . . My life is penetrated by the lives of other people and in turn penetrates their lives . . . so many interrelationships with other people with whom I am so closely connected . . . I live together with others and my life is inseparable from theirs . . .

7. My existence is a process of becoming — leading to meditation

From what have I developed? The first life on earth . . . The countless millions of organisms before man appeared . . . The people who have contributed to my being — two parents, four grandparents, eight great grandparents . . . All these have made me what I am . . .

What am I becoming? There are many different objectives in my life, but in which direction is it really moving? Am I on the way towards reaching the ultimate goal? Is my life directed towards fulfilling my essential being as a person? Or is it possible that I may only half-fulfil that aim or perhaps not fulfil it at all? . . . Will I, following the way of life that I am now following, really become what I intended to become? Or should I be developing along a different path? Is the ultimate mystery even greater? Am I moving towards an ultimate encounter? . . .

Meditating in this way, I try to be conscious of my life as a process of becoming. I try to experience myself as one who is constantly developing, moving, on the way . . . I then try to understand in what direction I am moving, what I am becoming, who I am becoming . . .

8. Demands are made on me — a text for guidance

The following text leads to meditation in a gradual ascent through recollection, reflection and re-experience. In this way, you can come to understand a part of the reality that you are and meditate about it.

I look for examples in the lives of other people which show the various ways in which demands have been made on those people although they have not been ordered or compelled to do what they have done. One obvious example is that of a mother with a sick child. Another is the case of a professor specializing in mathematics and insurance who heard of the pathetic attempts being made in a developing country to create a system of social security. Despite a successful career in the academic world, he felt that this demand was being made personally on him. In response to this call, he felt obliged to go. His wife was in agreement. There were certain serious misgivings with regard to their growing family, but they were overcome. He gave up his academic post and went to work in the Third World . . . The call had not come from any person or group of people. He simply offered himself . . .

Who made this demand on him? Life itself? If so, what does that mean? . . . Circumstances? But how could the circumstances of life have such power over a man living so far away that he feels called to give up his career, change his whole way of life and commit himself to people whom he does not know?

I look for an example in my own life which may be similar to this, a case in which I felt obliged . . . What made this demand on me? Who made this demand? A person? Was it a professional demand? Was it the situation that made the demand? . . . I explore the nature of the experience . . . I re-experience the call . . . I re-examine the way in which I responded . . . What is this deep-seated, tender yet urgent power in me, speaking to me through my conscience — then and now — and leaving me no peace until I respond to it? . . .

It is a power which is so compelling that it makes irresistible demands on me. I cannot go against it . . . I have no right to disregard it. Or even, in such cases, to have any control over myself. How is this? Is it that there are limits to my own rights imposed by those of my fellow men? That is part of the truth . . . But it goes beyond this — there is another power which makes such great demands on me. I am in a sense aware of the precise place where this demand first makes itself felt . . .

I experience myself as a person on whom demands are made. I am here for a reason . . . Although I am not sure precisely what that reason is . . . I am, however, sure that I am not here simply for myself. I am certainly not here for myself above all. What, then, am I here for?

I am conscious of something in me that corresponds to this

power of good that makes such demands on me . . . A desire, perhaps, to be committed . . . Sometimes this desire burns very low and then I feel empty, tired and sick of myself . . .

I am here for a reason. But what is that reason? I am certainly not here for only one thing or only one person. No one thing or person could ever have such total power over me. No one could demand total commitment on my part . . .

What is clear to me now is that by means of all these individual things and people one greater and all-embracing power breaks through. This power makes itself known to me via the individual things and people that I encounter and at the same time makes demands on me through them. It is present in everything that is good . . . It demands everything that is in me, the whole of me, my innermost self . . . At the same time it also entirely fills me and fulfils me. It refreshes me and strengthens me. It encourages me and makes me happy at the deepest level whenever I obey its call . . . I open myself to this power and submit myself to it. I ask that it will penetrate to my innermost being . . .

9. I am directed towards a 'you' — a text for guidance

I look for where this reality can be found in my life and in the lives of other people . . .

When I was a few months old, I must, like every baby, have smiled for the first time. This was brought about by my mother. She took me in her arms, fondled me, smiled at me and loved me. I responded . . . I wanted more and more to be with her . . .

Later on, my father entered my environment and influenced me in a different way. Then other children became important in my life — my brothers and sisters and other children in the neighbourhood and at school . . . In them and in the intimate relationships I enjoyed with them, I encountered another 'You'. In many ways, these relationships were closer and more accessible than those with my parents, but my parents' embrace was stronger . . .

The intimate relationship with them remained and continued to be deeply fulfilling. But as time passed its limitations became more apparent. My parents were no longer able to mean everything to me. I was in search of another and even closer relationship, another 'You' . . .

I look for friendship with others. I longed to be able to talk intimately to a friend who would listen to me, reply to me, understand and accept me, someone who was on equal terms with me . . . I recall the friendships I have had with other people . . . my first love affair . . . the first time I was fulfilled in love — and perhaps also disappointed . . . I remember these experiences and call them vividly to mind . . . Perhaps I am still looking, even now, for friendship. What am I really looking for? What will this intimate relationship with another, this 'You', really give me? . . .

(If you have experienced deep friendship or love in this way, you should ask yourself: what was the most profound aspect of the experience as a whole? You should reflect about the nature of the love relationship — being understood and accepted by the other person, being certain of the other, transcending oneself in love for the other, being in the other and his or her being in you. Meditate as deeply as possible about the experience of love as a whole and the mystery of that experience.)

But again there was the experience of the limitations of human friendship or love. The other can never completely understand me, never completely accept me and never love me totally for my own sake . . . There is always a residual lack of understanding in even the most intimate relationship, always some limitation . . . The other can never fully grasp the whole of me and can never completely acknowledge, love or heal me. This limitation in the love relationship is painful. Why is there this pain? . . . Love calls for total unity, but never quite finds it . . . What is the aim of love? What does it want? Towards what, towards whom is it directed?

My grace is precisely to be found in being aroused and in not being fulfilled. In loving another person and in being loved, I am made acutely aware of the deep reality of love, but at the same time I am painfully aware that the experience can never be ultimately fulfilling. It is not the ultimate reality in which I can completely transcend myself . . . My grace is precisely to be found in this . . .

I am conscious of the existence of a 'You' and know that this relationship will fulfil me. It is this ultimate 'You' whom I am seeking. My whole being is directed towards a relationship with this

'You' and always has been, even when I was looking for human friendship and love. A 'You' who understands me completely accepts me completely and brings this insatiable desire for love completely to rest, this longing that always ends in disappointment, that always falls short of the ideal, is rebuffed and has to accept only partial fulfilment. It is easy to understand why some people go from one person to another in search of love; finding it ultimately unsatisfying to pursue an intimate relationship with one person they tear themselves in two in relationships with more than one other . . .

In all this seeking, I know that I am looking for an encounter with the ultimate 'You'. If I allow room in myself, if I let this ultimate 'You' be what it really is in my innermost being, then I know that I am its counterpart and that this 'You' is very close to me. Our relationship is not marred by misunderstanding or lack of concern. It is all-embracing, excluding no part of me. It is totally accepting, rejecting nothing of my true self. It helps me to love where love seems impossible. It makes great demands on me, but gives me strength to respond. It never turns away from me in loathing, even if I hate myself. It shows itself above all as love, even when I am forgetful, tired or indifferent. It does not love some more attractive aspect of myself — it loves me totally. It completes what is lacking in me. It transcends me in every way and lets me participate in its own transcendent being. I long for this intimate relationship, which is the only one that is ultimately satisfying. It is this ultimate 'You' towards which I am directed. If I accept myself as I am . . . If I do not value myself too highly . . . If I do not misrepresent myself . . . If I want to become fully human . . . If I really want to become myself, I must move consciously towards this ultimate and all—embracing 'You' . . .

10. I live between hope and disappointment — leading to meditation

I begin by observing how I am always moving towards something . . . how I am always expecting something . . . always looking forward to the next day, the next activity, the next encounter . . . I live in expectation. I am constantly hoping — for a journey, for success, for promotion . . . I long for new friendship, for love . . . I take stock of this aspect of my life, this double cycle of hoping, expecting, achieving, having, passing and once again hoping . . . or if not achieving, being disappointed and hoping for something else . . .

What is the goal towards which this constant hoping in my life is moving? Is it something that is frequently never achieved and, when it is, is never really fulfilling? I let the real and all-embracing hope rise within me and observe it. I ask: what is its aim? If I were to allow this hope to be confined to the more limited goals in life, I would be doing violence to my true self. But it may be that everything that I have ever hoped for may provide a glimpse of the ultimately satisfying mystery behind all these individual goals. This underlying mystery is present and makes itself known in all my individual aims . . .

VII   OUR EXISTENCE — OPEN TO GOD

We all contain the promise of an unfathomable mystery. In meditation, it is important for us to plumb the depths of our being and thus to come into contact with this mystery.

In becoming aware of the presence of this mystery, we can learn to live as we should live. Our true lives are connected in so many ways and at so many points to this mystery. Meditating about this may open the way for us to a genuine inner revelation of this mystery, which is ultimately made explicit in the words and deeds of Jesus Christ, who has brought us the message of the living God.

In this chapter, I have tried to point to various existential data which are common to almost all of us, and at the same time to the different ways in which the ultimate mystery is made existentially known to us. Following the procedure you have used in the models so far provided in this book, you should consider each of the statements as a basis for meditation.

The statements can also be used as meditations about the nature of faith and about your own faith. If you do this, your personal relationship with God should gain in fulness and depth and your whole life ought to become increasingly open to the light of revelation.

I ask questions which go beyond and beneath the reality of this world.

The all-embracing meaning, the total and ultimate answer that makes itself known in all partial answers.

I look for what really matters.

The all-embracing value which makes itself visible in everything of value.

I think and my thoughts know no boundaries and seek the infinite.
I have to trust.

The prerequisite for such thoughts is the infinite.

That reality towards which my trust flows and which ultimately lets me trust.

I am full of desires and longings and experience these as a state of being directed towards something that is not in this world.

The real and ultimate objective of all my desires is discernible in all partial fulfilment which leaves me in the end unfulfilled or disappointed; it is what ultimately fulfils all desire.

I have in me a deep existential unrest.
I know, in moments of great love, that this love points beyond itself and the person I love to something that embraces my love and is ultimately supremely satisfying.

It is what brings true peace to my innermost being.
The reality which reveals itself in the experience of great love, through and beyond the one who is loved, as the ultimate objective of all love.

In addition to these positive experiences through which we can encounter the ultimate mystery of all being, we are also confronted with limitations, deficiencies and negative forces which can, surprisingly, perhaps, also provide access to this ultimate reality.

I have no security and am exposed to all risks.

The reality that provides ultimate security when everything that obviously belongs to this world fails.
The reality that is the opposite of nothing — the reality that is everything.

I know fear intimately — not fear of this or that person or thing, but the existential anxiety that makes me dread the empty void, nothing, the constant disappointment caused by the limitations of individual things.

I know what it is to be isolated in the midst of other people; I exist in a state of loneliness.

The power which overcomes my loneliness at all levels, which is with me in my innermost being and which, by its very nearness, 'consoles' me.

I have often been confronted with the meaninglessness of life.

The mystery that presents itself even in absurd situations as ultimate meaningfulness.

I have often experienced guilt and have judged and condemned myself.

The reality that accepts me even in my guilt and enables me to turn back and begin again.

I can find truth and greatness in extremely negative, even destructive situations.

The mystery that is the lasting foundation of man's life, even when everything else is taken from him.

I can find meaning and even greatness in selfless and even fruitless activity.

The one who stands up for me in giving himself up, who receives me in abandoning himself and who reveals himself as ultimate meaning; the one whom I in

the end encounter in selfless activity.

The whole of the Christian's existential meditation can be summarised in Augustine's statement: 'You have created us, God, for yourself and our hearts are restless until they rest in you'.

VIII   TAKING THE FUNDAMENTAL EXERCISE TO A DEEPER LEVEL

1.   Let go: your aim should be to let go of everything that is opposed to your true being. Above all, let go of your 'worldly' self which has developed in the course of your struggle for exist-ence and has falsified your 'essential' self. This 'worldly' self shows itself in many different ways — defensive attitudes, anxieties, infer-iority feelings, the wearing of protective masks, the playing of parts, ambition, self-assertion, projecting an image of oneself, aggressive behaviour and certain wrong moral attitudes such as untruthfulness and the absence of love.

In letting yourself go, you are preparing yourself to become free of the restrictions imposed by your small, 'worldly' self and to accept your true existence. Let yourself go in order to let God come to you. An unconscious lack of trust is expressed in this act of letting go. When you truly let yourself go, you give up all desire to think for yourself in an assertive way in the presence of God and all anxiety in your attitude towards him. Letting go thus opens the way to full trust in God and to complete self-abandonment.

2.   Sink down: this means that you are ready to go down to the depths of your being and to enter the ultimate existential sphere and be transformed by the experience. In sinking down, you are entrust-ing yourself to the original existence that God the creator wanted you to have.

The movement of sinking can, however, also go even deeper than this. The ground of your own being is borne up and suffused by an all-embracing Being. Sinking down into the lowest depths of your own being therefore also means moving into the ultimate ground of all being, entrusting yourself to that ground and becoming rooted in it.

3. Becoming one: there are many different meanings contained in these two short words. We can, for example, be 'outside ourselves' and we can 'come to ourselves'; we can be inwardly torn apart and we can also be 'at one' with ourselves. We may not necessarily be at one, our body and spirit perfectly united. In this fundamental exercise, we try to reach unity in an activity that embraces both aspects of our being — body and spirit. The decisive and guiding upper element, the spirit, should become one with our true being. This true being, which is so often suppressed or distorted by adversity, should in this way be allowed to expand and flourish. We can become one with the very source of life flowing from the ground of our being.

Becoming one means in the end becoming one with the mystery which Christians call God. It means becoming one with the Absolute which has been made known to us as holiness and love in Christ. It means being permeated with his spirit which reaches our innermost being. In this way, we shall be more and more transformed into the 'image of his Son' (Rom 8. 29).

4. Becoming new: We rise up, renewed, from these depths. The wheel of change, which has brought us from above to below and which has paused for a moment at its lowest point, now raises us up in renewed youthfulness and unity. Until we enter the next revolution and once again let go, sink down and become one and new.

The effects of this fundamental exercise are:
1.   It sets the deepest powers free and enables them to be effective.
2.   It frees us from the restrictions of self-centredness.
3.   It opens us to deeper realities.
4.   We practise the fundamental movement of all religious life.
5.   We come closer and closer to the ground of our real being.
6.   It sets the dynamism of our innermost being free and directs it towards its real and ultimate goal.

PART III

CHRISTIAN MEDITATIONS

I INTRODUCTION

When a Christian meditates, natural meditation is frequently suffused with faith. The Christian will inevitably see God's creation in nature and he will see God the creator in that creation and his brothers in Christ in his fellow men.

Although both kinds of meditation are often intermingled, they can be distinguished. Whereas every human being is capable of meditating naturally, it is only the believing Christian who can properly carry out Christian meditation.

The Christian who meditates knows, because of the good news of Christ, that God is looking for him. He knows that God is love and that his goal is to penetrate into this love of God, to live with God and to become more and more with him. Moving constantly towards God, his aim is above all 'to comprehend . . . what is the breadth and length and height and depth' of God's work of salvation, in which God wishes to make all men at one with himself in Christ. He seeks 'to know the love of Christ which surpasses knowledge' and to be 'filled with all the fulness of God' (Eph 3. 18-19). Whenever he fails in this aim, he will find comfort in the knowledge that 'love will find a way', his love for God and God's love for him.

On this way, he should also find the following rules helpful:

1. Do not underestimate the importance of the natural meditations in the first and second parts of this book. The point of departure for almost all these meditations is some concrete reality of human experience in which God has situated us. They also lead to a deepening of our humanity, which should become, through these exercises, more open to receive God. They also frequently lead to meditations about faith.

2. Continue to use the fundamental exercise. This leads, in a unique and quite direct way, into the depths at which meditation takes place. At the same time, it also opens up a whole world of interior experience. If it is practised at a deeper and Christian

level, so that it plunges into the 'Spirit of the Son' who is in us, it will take us down to an even deeper level of unity with God. In Christian meditation proper, it can best be used alternately with meditations on biblical texts.

3.   If you really want to penetrate to the heart of God's word and allow it to have its full effect on you, you may find it best to follow the 'bowl movement' outlined earlier in this book. To recapitulate and develop what was said there, you should begin by considering the material selected for meditation externally and superficially and then in stages press gently forward from outside and above to within and below. Your aim should be to proceed from the surface of the matter and to penetrate to its centre and its depth. When you have reached this central depth, you should remain there motionless for as long as possible. On the other hand, the movement from consideration to meditation is also valuable. In other words, you can begin by listening, examining, comparing, reflecting and applying — states in which you will be more active — and then go on to being astonished, touched, seized, held and filled with God. At this second stage, you will be more receptive and God will, with his Spirit, be more active. These two processes are different, but sometimes they overlap, alternate or mingle with each other. Remember at all times that you should remain still whenever anything touches you deeply and stay with that experience for as long as you find it beneficial.

4.   If certain words or phrases suggest themselves to you during meditation and these can easily be repeated, do not attempt to suppress them or drive them out. You should on the contrary use them and repeat them, since they will help you to recall the reality with which they were associated, to keep it present in your mind and become one with it.

5.   If your Christian meditation is to develop, you will have to make use of the conversions and clarifications demanded by the gospel. These often occur of their own accord during meditation, but the following may help you to grasp them and make them your own:

Make God the architect of your life; he plans and designs the structure of our lives and we fit into that plan.

Make yourself entirely dependent on God's guidance.

Regard God's will as the ultimate value.

Make God's way of thinking your own and try to recognize and then carry out his wishes and intentions.

Do not attempt to be good in God's presence; be poor in his presence and be good with him and through him.

Do not at any time be closed to God; be open to his Spirit and allow him to fashion your innermost self.

Carry out the stages of love of your neighbour, especially by making his interests your own and by doing everything in order to overcome conflict and to achieve reconciliation and forgiveness.

Have faith in God's love, which seeks out and is merciful and always available.

Expose yourself totally to that love without any reservation.

6.   Continue to meditate. Do it every day. Go on all your life. Never lose heart and give up. Every time you fall down, get up and go on. God is always forgiving and will always reach us, wherever we are. He can 'raise up children to Abraham' from stones (Mt 3. 9). He is also able 'by the power at work within us to do far more abundantly than all that we ask or think' (Eph 3. 20).

Depending on the stage which you have reached in the development of your life of faith and prayer, you will want to choose, from the examples that follow, what suits you and what lends itself in your particular case to fruitful meditation.

II   MATERIALS AND ACTIVITIES

1. The stream of gifts and tasks – leading to meditation

The following texts should help you to meditate at a deep level about your own experience and to become conscious of the one from whom everything that is good comes and who provides us with tasks in life.

The material

Every day countless things take place in our lives. Sometimes these things come as gifts — water, light, meals, encounters with other people and so on — and at other times they come as tasks — work, difficulties, opposition, and so on. Both, however, can be places where we meet, in intimate encounter, the ultimate 'You'.

Paths to meditation

The statements that follow may be sufficient for some readers to achieve a deep level in meditation. Others may feel the need for a gradual approach.

1.   Try to find complete peace at the end of the day, in the evening. Then let the events of the day pass slowly and peacefully through your mind, remember them as precisely as possible and observe and recognize everything that was good. The next step is to halt at certain particular points and be alert to the fact that all these good things are gifts. Pause for a longer time over certain of these gifts, be glad about them and think: given . . . to me . . . from him . . . from you . . . The words 'from you' can be repeated as a prayer of thanksgiving and recognition.

2.   Use the fundamental exercise to become completely quiet and relaxed at the beginning of the day, in the morning. Then review in your mind the good things that you will experience during the day — warmth, clothing, your home, breakfast, meetings with people you know . . . Think about all these good experiences and say to yourself: they are taking place in my life; they are given to me. Experience this as deeply as possible, this sense of being given . . . Pause for as long as possible in this stream of gifts which comes to you from God's love. The feeling can be expressed in words: to me . . . from you . . .

3.   In the evening, look back at the events of the day and ask yourself: what are the tasks that have confronted me today? What demands have been made on me by this situation or by that situation? What have I to do? . . . Then respond to all these demands: I have been given the task of . . . by him . . . by you . . . Finally, try to find what God's intentions have been for you throughout the whole of the day . . . Or simply rest in the stream of tasks . . .

4.   In the morning, look forward to the day ahead. Ask yourself: What tasks lie ahead today? What will my tasks be in my encounters with other people . . . professionally . . . in other spheres . . . You

may like to repeat as a prayer: What are your intentions for me today? What do you expect from me? Be aware of the stream of tasks and of what lies behind that stream — the one from whom everything that is good comes, all tasks, all the things that have to be done, all the obstacles that have to be overcome, all the goals that we should aim at and try to reach . . . Another prayer that you could repeat is: For you . . . Everything can be seen by him . . . I will try to do everything in his service, everything according to his intention.

5.   The more you think about them in this way, the more clearly you will be able to see the events of your daily life in the light of his intention . . . the more clearly you will be able to understand your experience as a continuous gift. Everything that is good will become an encounter with his giving and therefore with his love. You will become more and more alert to his intention for you in the things that happen to you every day. You will become increasingly aware of the meaning of the words 'from you' in your encounter with these gifts. You will see with increasing clarity, when you carry out your everyday tasks, that they are 'from you'.

His presence will break through the events of your daily life. Nothing will remain outside him or apart from him. All the things and events that take place in your life will become places where you meet his giving and his intentions.

If you learn in this way to look at the stream of gifts and tasks that comes from God, to understand it correctly and to live in it and from it, your relationship with God will become varied and rich. The meditations that result from the experience of God's presence will increase in number and variety.

2. I experience: 'created' — leading to meditation

The texts that follow shoud give access to a very wide field of Christian meditation. As time passes, this ought also to be expanded by the addition of new material and deeper and more intensive experience. If you persist thus, you should pass into the very heart of this experience of meditation, where you are transformed and, indeed, 'created'.

The material

The world of man and nature is full of forms that have not been made by man and of functions that have not been invented by man. Let this fact have its ultimate effect on you and it will lead you into a state of astonishment, to a meditation about the underlying mystery and to a venture into the unknown. An ultimate reality will become visible to the believer, who will experience in the world and in himself — created.

Ways to meditation

Many people will be able to meditate about this simple theme without needing any steps leading to meditation as such. They will be able to pause, confronted by the created world, or by the fact: I am created . . . I am here because it is your will . . .

Anyone who is looking for actual steps, can make a selection from the following suggestions:

1.   Let your gaze wander over your experience of man's existence and as soon as you are conscious of 'created' let it rest quietly there . . .

2.   In a state of recollection consider a plant, a flower in the garden, a tree or an animal and let yourself be touched by its existence. In meditation, you will see the thing as a form. This means: formed. Going further, this means: formed by someone, formed by one who forms.

3.   Our point of departure can also be one particular phenomenon in ourselves. We have all experienced at some time or other that our own breathing functions as it were independently. Be conscious of it now, experience it slowly and meditatively — it is a function which was not instituted by me, not created by me . . . Something very similar can be experienced in feeling your own pulse . . . in looking at your own hand . . . We can move it and experience its movement and its functions, but we can seldom know how it is that it moves. Its function was not instituted by me. It is something that is given to me . . . It is created . . .

4.   In the same way, it is possible to go through the whole of your body, beginning with your head . . . with your eyes . . . your ears . . . your mouth . . . down to your feet . . . Perceive all these parts of your

body, experience them as deeply as possible and, while you are doing this, be conscious of the fact that they are: created ... by you ...

We can experience something very similar when we look at nature . . when we contemplate the countryside . . . technical apparatus, tools, machinery and the materials from which they were made . . . The materials existed, but were refashioned . . .

5.   Meditation about 'created' can be deepened if we take as our subject a loving encounter: here am I and there is the other and we both fit so well together . . . Similarly, we can look at a newly born baby: everything is there and the baby is alive, but was not created by us . . . Finally, everything that we know in the world has something of this 'created' aspect.

6.   Everything can ultimately be brought together into a total experience: Here am I . . . and this . . . created . . . by you . . .

3. Living subject to God's guidance — texts leading to meditation

The central reality

In Christian meditation, we have no need to restrict ourselves simply to our own, often unsatisfactory experiences. We can always enter the great stream of man's experience of God which begins in the Bible. God can be seen in scripture as communicating himself to man and actively looking for him, forgiving him and loving him. If we participate in these great experiences described in the Bible and live with them, we shall certainly discover for ourselves their deep truthfulness and reliability.

It is clear from scripture and other Christian sources that man is directed towards life with God. He has therefore to live subject to God's guidance. If he lives in this way, he will give up all false and presumptuous claims to independence and accept gladly the generous offer of potential growth that God, his loving partner, makes to him. He will in this way come to resemble a mason who decides to abandon a frantic cutting and laying of stones and to place himself at the disposal of the architect of the cathedral and thus become a fellow-builder of the great pile. We need have no fear of doing this with God. He knows us better than we know ourselves. He loves us infinitely. He also knows better than we do how to use our environment and our own possibilities for our own good.

Steps in meditating about this mystery

These steps should be used again and again in order to initiate ourselves into life subject to God's guidance. If we persist in the following exercises, we should find that God will guide more and more irresistibly, permeate our spirit more and more fully and transform us more and more deeply.

1.   We say, again and again, the words 'Thy will be done'. At the same time, we look honestly at our life, our possibilities and our tasks, with the deep desire to know what God's intention is for us and what he thinks of our life. In this way, we hand over to him in a fundamental but concrete manner, the guidance of our life, its plan and all decisions.

2.   We repeat the prayer: 'Show me your intention for me'. We long to know what that intention is and to reach the level of his plan for us and we ask for God to reveal it to us in the events of our life and to enable us to achieve it.

3.   We make ourselves completely subject to his guidance. We cease to see our life simply from our own point of view, to plan it independently and to try to achieve our own intentions. We know that he will guide us, on the one hand in the external situations in our life in which we receive gifts or have demands made on us, and, on the other, in our inner life, in which we experience the tender and illuminating presence of his Spirit.

4.   Meditation and living become more and more deeply one. Reflecting about texts taken from the Bible will help us to have a deeper understanding of his intentions. Our failures and shortcomings call for repentance, conversion and a new beginning. Conformity with the will of God leads us towards increasing unity with the Infinite.

4. God sees, calls us, waits, hears and invites us – leading to meditation

Meditation should be simple and it should be repeated. It should be felt in our experiences. Without losing its simplicity and its unity, simple meditation can still be developed. As an example of this, we will consider how God sees us.

A possible point of departure is to call to mind and reflect about occasions when a particular person has seen us and looked at us in a special way. If it helps, write down this experience . . .

There are two ways of carrying out this meditation:

(a) I adopt the exterior and interior attitude of meditation and think of God as great and loving. I know that he sees me. I let his gaze rest on me.

(b) Before beginning to meditate, I think about certain aspects of this meditative procedure. His gaze is my salvation . . . He looks at me because he wants to save me . . . I give myself up to him . . . I open myself to him . . . Looking at me, he discovers values in me that I and others overlook . . . He uncovers aspects of my being, like a doctor uncovering a wound . . . What I cover up or repress, he sees . . . But his gaze is merciful; he wants to help me, to heal me and to save me . . . He sees my aim . . . He sees me . . . He sees what I may become, his intention for me, where he wants to lead me . . . I want to remain in his gaze . . . This material should lead to various meditations.

The same can be done with other aspects of God's activity with us: He calls me . . . He waits for me . . . He hears me . . . He invites me . . . (how? to do what?) This procedure can be extended, for example, by thinking: God seeks me out . . . He follows me . . . (Why? what does he want from me?) These meditations can be supplemented by words taken from the psalms or by recalling corresponding experiences with our fellow-men. Do any particularly relevant experiences come to mind?

Remember the basic rule — select no more than one theme and penetrate more and more deeply into this. Do not allow yourself to be disturbed by other themes.

5. Because God looks at me and speaks to me, I come to life — leading to meditation

We would not be ourselves, we would never 'come to life' if other people did not notice us, look at us, speak to us and give us a place in their lives. We would never have come to life in the past if this had never happened.

Themes of this meditation:

I.   God is the one who looks at me and speaks to me and thus makes me come to life.

II.   Who have I become by having been looked at and spoken to by God?

I.   For this first theme, we look for experiences with our fellow men. We look in the sphere of interpersonal relationships and try to experience again what happened as we matured and became more fully human by being looked at and spoken to by others. Let us consider some examples of this. If a baby is treated like a thing when it is being fed or dressed, it will behave like a thing. If his mother looks at him, smiles and speaks to him, he will come to life. A child at school who doesn't quite succeed in work and with his school-fellows will soon give up and switch off. As soon as he begins to succeed and to be accepted, is seen and is spoken to, he will come to life. A girl at a dance — if the boys look at her and ask her to dance, she soon comes to life. A young person at a meeting may speak and the people may listen to him and take him seriously. After the meeting, someone may perhaps address him. This more personal contact will increase his sense of being someone. A quiet, retiring girl student is seen after the lecture by the lecturer, who speaks to her. At once she feels lifted up out of the anonymous mass of students and is grateful to have been addressed. A young couple begin to call each other by their Christian names and experience a new coming to life . . . We should enter into these experiences as deeply as if they were our own.

II.   These interpersonal relationships which we or others have experienced can now be applied to our relationship with God. We say: 'You have regarded the low estate of your handmaiden (Lk 1. 48) and God says: 'I have called you by name' (Is 43. 1). Many other quotations from scripture could be found with a similar theme, that of God's looking at us and listening to us.

What kind of standing must I have in God's sight, for him to look at me? . . . He must look at me as he looked at Mary (Lk 1. 48) . . .

I try to let his looking become a reality for me. What happens to me as a result of his looking at me? In what way does it build me up? . . . Being looked at by God gives me peace, strength, a sense of well-being and security . . .

He addresses me most intimately, as a close friend . . . When he speaks to me, what he says penetrates to my innermost being . . . I let his speaking to me remain within me, as deeply as possible . . . for as long as possible . . . What can hardly be understood becomes clear — God brings each one of us to life; we mean something to him . . . He is love and whoever loves says to the other who is loved: You mean something to me . . . You are important to me . . . It is clear what faith in God really means. It is not simply accepting God's existence. It is knowing intimately and in the depth of our being that God looks at us and speaks to us . . . that I mean something to him . . . that he makes me the person I am really able to become . . . or am . . . He builds me up . . . I try to expose myself as much as possible and to open myself to the effect that his looking at me, speaking to me and loving me has . . . I look for the best way to respond to it and to allow myself to be changed by it . . .

6. 'Hear O Israel' (Deut 6. 4-9) — leading to meditation

The text

'Hear, O Israel: The Lord our God is one; and you shall love the Lord your God with all your heart, and with all your soul, and with all your might. And these words, which I command you this day shall be upon your heart; and you shall teach them diligently to your children, and shall talk of them when you sit in your house, and when you walk by the way, and when you lie down, and when you rise. And you shall bind them as a sign upon your hand, and they shall be as frontlets between your eyes. And you shall write them on the doorposts of your house and on your gates'.

Reflecting about the past

Before we can properly reflect and meditate about this text, we must call vividly to mind what lay behind it — its prehistory.

1.   The Israelites looked forward to salvation from the Egyptian army. They were mortally afraid. Everything that they valued was threatened — their possessions, their cattle, their women and children, their own skins . . . The enemy was close on their heels and would soon catch up with them and put them to death. Their fear embraced the whole of their lives and paralysed their will to love and to desire . . . Yet it gave way to another and stronger experience — a sense of liberation. In every aspect of their existence they became aware of the power of God. This power penetrated everything . . . Think about this experience of the Israelites, enter into it as fully as you can, apply it to yourself . . .

2.   This God of great power then led the Israelites through the wilderness, letting them suffer hunger and thirst there and be exposed to danger. Finally, he revealed himself in his transcendent power on Mount Sinai. 'You have seen what I did to the Egyptians, and how I bore you on eagles' wings and brought you to myself . . . All the earth is mine . . . Take heed that you do not go up into the mountain or touch the border of it; whoever touches the mountain shall be put to death'. (Exod 19. 4, 5, 12; see also Deut 5. 22-23). Let God's power have its effect on you.

Consideration of the text

The God who is so powerful in the exodus from Egypt and the time spent in the desert is at the same time the God whom we can love in the text 'Hear, O Israel'. His total power, from which we shrink back in dread, is changed into a total attraction: 'You shall love the Lord your God . . .'

You should try to understand this change. Meditate about it and try to make it your own . . .

2.   This commandment to love God should have the most profound effect on us. It should set everything in us in motion, stir the depths of our being and direct us powerfully towards God, so that we surrender ourselves completely to him, loving him 'with all our heart, with all our soul, and with all our might'.

(a)   This self-surrender is naturally — and rightly — directed towards many different things and people — those whom we love, our possessions, our tasks . . . But what we are commanded to do in these words of the Old Testament is to surrender ourselves totally,

from the depths of our being. This total love will overflow all other love for things and people in this world and flow irresistibly on towards God, meeting him wherever he is to be found . . . Understand this as deeply as you can and make it your own.

(b) This self-surrender to God should include everything in you: 'You shall love God with all your heart'. 'With all your might' you should listen, think, act, grow and develop, desire, fashion your life and shape the world according to God's will. In all this, you will be expressing a love that is in accordance with God's plan for you . . . Meditate peacefully about all these different aspects, and about the whole procedure.

3. The whole of this commandment cannot be accomplished in a single hour or so. The commandment clearly applies to the whole of your life — the very words of the text indicate this — and to every level of your daily experience. It has therefore to be carried out with a total self-surrender to God and his will and a total resolution to make it effective in every aspect of your being. Read the text again carefully and examine the language used: 'These words . . . shall be upon your heart'; 'talk of them'; wear them 'as frontlets'; 'write them'; . . . These words of the commandment to love must be with you everywhere and in all the circumstances of your life: 'in your house'; 'when you walk'; 'when you lie down'; 'when you rise' . . . 'upon your hand'; 'between your eyes'; 'on the doorposts of your house' and 'on your gates' . . . You must never forget them . . . You must always live in the presence of God's words and indeed of God himself, the great and powerful yet loving God . . . You must constantly surrender yourself to him, living at one with him, yet distinct from him. That is the only normal existence which is in accordance with his plan.

Words of personal prayer may suggest themselves

Who are you, God, coming forward to meet us in your divinity? . . . shattering all our preconceptions and norms? . . . making such excessive demands on us? . . . Or is this your way of giving us immeasurable grace? . . . Is it possible for me to understand in this way the extent to which you are God? . . .

Your demand for total love and self-surrender on my part must be the ultimate meaning of your work of redemption. Your sending of the Spirit also makes it possible for me to achieve what is demanded of me and to do what is in accordance with your will for me . . .

Deeper meditation

Go back to this text, read it again and again, consider all its details, see it as a whole, carry out what it tells you to do, make it your own . . . Go further and meditate about God himself, the living God and move patiently into a living relationship with him.

7. The forgiving father (Lk 15. 16-32) —leading to meditation

What is the ultimate mystery of our existence, the reality we call God, really like? What is his attitude towards me? Many people cannot find an answer to these and similar questions in the Old Testament. They find such answers more easily in the gospels.

There are so many excellent texts in the New Testament that we shall consider only four examples of how to proceed from a reading to a meditation. The first is the story of the forgiving father.

The procedure

First of all, read the text slowly and carefully, if possible aloud and, if you wish, together with other people.

Then ask yourself: What is said to us in this text? What is the purpose of the text? How does it concern us and our lives? What is its central message?

In silence, after the reading, penetrate to the heart of the theme. Put yourself as completely as possible in the position of the son who left his father's house and experience what he experienced, especially his distress, his longing to go home, his reception when he arrived . . .

Then let the whole experience become a way of understanding God and our relationship with him. He waits till I return home to him. He longs for me to come back and draws me to him. He receives me and accepts me as I am. He forgives me completely, without a word of reproach. He is glad and loving. All I have to do is to entrust myself to him without reservation . . .

The meditation proper will begin at the point where the Father accepts. Remain at this point. God accepts me as I am. In order to remain quietly here, let yourself go, let your breathing be as relaxed as possible, wait patiently. Be alert and open to this profound reality and let it enter you and take control of you . . .

After practising this exercise, a student wrote: 'The whole time, I felt the Father's hand on my back'. She had found the centre and the depth of this experience and had remained in it.

8. The lost drachma (Lk 15. 8-10) — leading to meditation

God not only waits for us and accepts us as we are. He looks for us. That is the theme of this parable.

The procedure

Read the text slowly and if possible aloud. I imagine a woman, kneeling on the earth floor of a house in Palestine. She has swept the floor. Now she looks carefully through the pile of dust in the corner until she finds the coin. Smiling with happiness, she stands up . . .

This is a picture of God's seeking love. In that love, God revealed himself in Christ, who humbled himself, looked for us, did not turn away from our dirt and with joy found us . . .

I see myself as the lost coin and I meditate about the action carried out by God, who comes down to my level, picks me up out of the dirt and finds me with great joy. This whole procedure can only be grasped adequately as a picture and in meditation . . . I experience the joy of being sought and found and thank God for it.

9. Jesus cures a blind man — leading to meditation

Jesus' actions tell us in a different way what we are told in the parables. What follows is a detailed procedure of how to use a description of such an action, in this case the cure of a blind man, in meditation.

The text: (Mk 8. 22-26)

The scene (the upper and outside ring of the bowl movement)

The main street of Bethsaida. A side street goes down to the right.
Houses. Washing hung out to dry. Below, part of the lake is visible.
A boat on the shore. Nets drying. People are seen coming. Two men
are leading another man, who seems to be blind.

The external procedure (the next ring of the bowl movement)

Jesus, in the street, sees the men approaching . . . They come up to
him and ask him . . . He takes the blind man by the hand . . . He
leads him out of the village . . . off the road, where there are some
bushes . . .

   He spreads spittle over the blind man's eyes (clear sign language)
. . . He lays his hands on him (a gesture of blessing) . . . Then he
asks him: 'Do you see anything?' . . . Something has taken place in
the man, through the signs . . . 'I see men . . . I can see something
moving around . . . They look like trees.' . . . One more step and
the cure is completed: 'Then again he laid his hands upon his eyes;
and he looked intently and was restored, and saw everything clearly'.
The man is cured.

   'And he sent him away to his home, saying: "Do not even enter
the village" '. Jesus did not want him to be shaken out of this
deep experience by an encounter with the people of the village and
their excited talk. Peace reigns . . . Discretion.

The inner experience (the third ring of the bowl movement)

We penetrate into the inner depth of the events that have taken
place: seeing the men approaching . . . their request . . . taking the
blind man by the hand . . . Jesus' relaxed, natural humanity . . .
leading him away . . . a quiet place, away from the crowd . . . discretion . . . Without any distractions and in a state of complete
recollection, the man experiences God's intervention, the effects
of his saving power.

   The signs and, in them, the inner experience. The cure — Yahweh's intervention in his life through the medium of this prophet. . .
But the blind man also has an inner, spiritual experience. The first
step: he begins to see. The transformation begins to take place,
through this man Jesus . . . The second step: A second laying on of

hands and the cure is completed . . . The new level of existence: seeing. The world and all that it contains begins to penetrate . . . Life is open to many new contacts . . . A gift from the living God . . . An experience of his all-embracing power, his benevolence, his presence . . . I have been personally touched and cured by him . . . I can see! What a great gift!

The third step: the inner experience of encounter with God . . . Not in the village, but in seclusion . . . a quiet assimilation of what has happened . . . not overwhelmed by the excitement of the people or persuaded by them that there has been no cure or inner transformation . . .

The meditation (the inner depth of the bowl movement)

Here are some suggestions which can be used as points of departure for a gradual transition into meditation proper: Jesus taking the blind man by the hand . . . taking me by the hand . . . Jesus addressing the blind man personally . . . speaking intimately to me . . . I become conscious of my own blindness . . . my blindness to God's intentions . . . to the needs of other people . . . to opportunities to do good . . . to the inner light . . . 'What do you want me to do for you?' The two blind men called to Jesus on the way out of Jericho: 'Lord, let our eyes be opened' (Mt 20. 32). Let my eyes be opened, Lord, to you, to other people, to the signs of the times, to myself . . . Stay in the Lord's presence . . . He alone can give me eyes of faith, the eyes of love, an inner vision of the great power and love of God . . . Let his light penetrate as deeply as possible into your innermost being.

The steps indicated in this procedure, in which the bowl movement is used, can, of course, be followed in many other meditations about biblical scenes. It is, however, important to be free. Many people who are just beginning may find it helpful initially to distinguish the steps quite clearly from each other and later to let them merge into each other. For other people, this is disturbing and they will naturally prefer to combine the inner experience and the meditation proper. Many people, already advanced in meditative techniques, will begin to meditate even while they are reading the text.

10. The great catch of fish — leading to meditation

The text (Lk 5. 1-11)

The procedure

The bowl movement can also be used here. We can proceed from the
upper, outer edge to the centre and the depth of meditation.

First read the text slowly and carefully. Then, bearing the external
procedure as a whole well in mind, ask yourself questions, especially
about the significance of the whole passage and about what it says
personally to you. A commentary is useful here. If you are meditating in a group, a quiet discussion will help. In this way, you will
become more and more conscious of the inner experience.

There is one incident in the story which can lead us to a particularly deep level: Peter's falling down before Jesus. Reflection
about this action of Peter's should make you move to a state of
recollection and deep experience in the bowl movement. Like Moses
before the burning bush, Peter falls down in front of Jesus. He senses
that he is in the presence of Yahweh, who is active in Jesus in this
event . . . He knows that there is some aspect of him that is not in
accordance with Jesus . . . I am not really at one with him, he
thinks . . . But Jesus raises him up from the depths of humility. In
future, cured of all complacency, he will be catching not fish, but
men . . .

The meditation

Peter's experience, his encounter with the presence of God in Jesus,
his shattering, revolutionary inner transformation, in which he
becomes a different person . . . Experience this yourself as deeply
as possible.

You may be helped in this meditation by the following suggestions: Peter before Jesus . . . I see myself in front of Jesus. What can
I boast about in his presence? I am poor . . . But have I let go of
everything? Am I really in the depths of humility? So that he can

raise me up, cured? I remain in this deep experience and let myself be transformed as he looks at me. I do nothing. His gaze penetrates into my innermost being and changes me.

11. Christ fulfils our deepest desires — leading to meditation

A good way of achieving a living relationship with Christ is to take your personal desires in life as your point of departure and try to understand how these are fulfilled by Christ. You should find the following text useful.

It is divided into three steps. The first step is to recognize that the desires mentioned below are present in all of us; sometimes we are conscious of them, sometimes we do not confess them to ourselves. You should let them rise up inside you, confess to yourself that they are there, savour them and accept them. At the second step, think about the way in which Christ fulfils each of these desires. In this reflection, you may be able to recall relevant places in the Bible. Do this before looking up the passages given below.

At the third step, you should allow Christ to fulfil the desires and longings that have formed the subject of your reflection. Let them grow into Christ like roots growing into the soil. You may find it helpful to pray aloud at this stage, confessing in words that you have these desires, that you trust him and give yourself up totally to him and that you want him to become the goal and the fulfilment of the deepest desires of your life. In this way, your whole life will become rooted in him.

The reader must decide for himself whether he prefers to meditate about one of these desires every day or about several. To stay for a fairly long time at each of the three steps in turn certainly facilitates the transition to meditation proper.

The following desires are present in us:

I want to be understood (Mk 12. 43)

to be recognized (Jn 1. 47; 4. 17-18; Rev 2. 19)

to learn how to live properly (Mt 22. 16)

to have an aim in life that is worth striving to achieve (Phil 3. 12-14)

to know the way (Jn 14. 6)

to possess something that is not simply temporary (Mt 6. 19ff)

to be loved without self-interest (Gal 2. 20)
to be able to love without throwing myself away (Jn 21. 15-17)
to be secure and protected (Mt 23. 27)
to be certain (Jn 10. 29)
to be unconquerable (Jn 16. 33; Acts 5. 41-42; Jn 5. 4)
I would like a really trustworthy friend (Jn 15. 15)
a friend who is always ready to listen to me (Mt 11. 28)
who always understands me (Lk 7. 44-47)
who wants me to prosper (Rom 8. 28)
who reveals my mistakes to me (Mt 5-7)
who makes me happy (Jn 17. 13)
who supports me (Rom 8. 38-39)
who never disappoints me (Mt 7. 24-25)
who does not deceive me (Heb 10. 23)
who looks for my friendship (Rev 3. 8)
who is happy about my love (Rev 3. 20)
I would like a Lord and Master to whom I can look up (Jn 6. 68)
who does not overlook my faults (Rev 2. 4)
who makes demands on me (Lk 9. 57-62)
who insists that I should be a whole person (Rev 3. 15-16)
who helps me to overcome my faults (Phil 4. 13; 2 Cor 12. 9)
who gives me a guarantee that I shall be successful (Jn 8. 12)
who sets me free from boredom and annoyance (1 Cor 13. 5-7)
who liberates me from the narrowness of existence (Jn 10. 16)
who gives meaning to my life (Jn 17. 3)
who teaches me to understand the world (Mt 6. 26; 13. 24-30)
who provides me with a plan for my life (Eph 1. 18-23)
who helps me to become what I am intended to be (1 Tim 1.15)
who brings out the best in me (Mt 5. 48; Phil 1. 6)
who helps me to be faithful (1 Tim 1. 12)
who enables me not to worry (Mt 6. 25-34)
who changes everything that is unpleasant in me into good
(Acts 5. 41)
who makes me inwardly rich (Eph 3. 8-9)
who makes me strong (Rom 8. 37; Phil 4. 13)
who makes me popular (Acts 2. 47)
who enables me to transcend myself (Rom 8. 14, 29)
I would like one who is greater than I am (Mt 10. 37)

whom I can admire (Lk 11. 27)
who is influential (Jn 1. 9; 12. 32)
who calls me to a great task (Mt 11. 12; Lk 11. 23)
who is powerful (Mt 28. 18)
who can change the world (Rev 21. 5)
behind whom many stand (Rev 5. 9)
whose plan embraces the whole world (Lk 1. 33; Eph 1. 10;1 Cor
15. 28)
who brings peace (Jn 4. 27; Acts 2. 42-47; 4. 32)
who puts me in the right place (Eph 4. 11-13)
who fulfils me (Jn 11. 25)
who makes me happy (Rev 19. 9).

Transition to meditative prayer

Most of the above desires can be repeated as prayers (see p. 109).
They can also be used to deepen your experience of life in the form
of the rosary of Christ. This is practised in the following way. You
must first learn the Christ prayer given below by heart. When you
use this prayer, add after the words 'our Lord and saviour' one of
the desires listed above, for example: 'who never disappoints me' or
'who makes me inwardly rich'. The Christ prayer is as follows:
    We praise you, Lord Jesus Christ,
    Son of the living God.
    You are the redeemer of the world,
    our Lord and saviour.
    Come, Lord, and help us,
    so that we may live with you for ever
    and enter the kingdom of your Father. Amen.

12. Christ in three events and us – a basic suggestion

It is not possible for us always to bear in our hearts and minds
everything in the life and activity of our Lord. We need places in
his life to which we can return again and again, where we can stay
and meditate and from which we can draw sustenance. These places
must, however, be central in Christ's life and they must have a very
important meaning for us. They may, of course, be different places

for each one of us. If we were, however, to name three such places which are a constant source of love, renewal and union with God for most Christians, these would undoubtedly be the washing of the disciples' feet, the crucifixion and the sending of the Spirit.

The first of these belongs to the first stage of Christ's life — to his public life of preaching and teaching. He is active in this event. He humbles himself and performs a selfless service. He says: 'You also ought to wash one another's feet' (Jn 13. 14). This is a simple instruction and we can easily hear in it the Lord's own attitude and selfless love . . .

Christ's suffering and death on the cross belongs to the second stage of his life. In it, his whole life is, as it were, focussed at a single point — he bears witness to God and his word, he glorifies the Father and he gives himself to him in obedience and love and is absolute and selfless love for us. It is obvious that we should meditate as often as possible about the crucifixion. On the cross, Christ does not turn away from those who crucify him. He looks at us and stretches out his arms to us in love . . .

The third of these events, the sending of the Spirit, belongs to the third stage of Christ's life, his glorification. The risen Christ communicates his Spirit to us. He enables us, by giving us the Spirit, to share in his innermost life, his attitude towards God and man, his sonship and his joy (Jn 15. 11) and peace (Jn 14. 27).

These three events that occurred at different stages in the life of our Lord can certainly help to make our union with him more personal, our love for him more profound and our openness to and our service of our fellow men more sincere. We can indeed learn, by meditating frequently and deeply about them, to live fully in and through Christ.

13. We meditate about Jesus Christ — a fundamental direction

Nowhere else has God come so close to us as he did in Jesus. 'For there is one God and there is one mediator between God and men, the man Jesus Christ' (1 Tim 2. 5). He is therefore bound to be at the very centre of our meditation as Christians. The following six directions are fundamental. They should help to point the way through the many different materials used along the road of meditation.

1.   It is of fundamental importance to learn more and more about Jesus in his earthly life. We therefore read the gospels and learn about him in the scenes depicted there: his journeys, his encounters with people, his words, his prayer, his suffering and his death. We also use all the means available to help us to reach a better understanding of the earthly life of our Lord — commentaries, maps, illustrations and so on.

2.   This leads to an imitation of Christ.

(a)   We listen to his word. We do not simply get to know what he said. We let his word speak to us personally. We let it penetrate to our innermost being. We allow ourselves to be gripped and overwhelmed by it. We direct our lives in accordance with his word and live by it. We accept, for example, his word concerning the coming kingdom of God and we try to live in the spirit of the Sermon on the Mount.

(b)   We follow his example. He is our Lord and Master. We are his disciples. We imitate above all his total obedience to God's will. 'My food is to do the will of him who sent me' (Jn 4. 34). We try especially to follow him in the example of his life with God and for God, in his life for other men, in his openness to everyone and in his patient endurance to the end. We contemplate Jesus Christ in all that he said and did. We are changed by all this and we try to imitate him.

3.   Christ lives. It is by looking at the Lord in his life on this earth that he is given form and colour and that he is brought close to us as a man. He and his life become part of our own experience. But the events of that life took place almost two thousand years ago. Christ was, however, raised from the dead and now he lives. We look up to the living and exalted Christ. In this way, we are like Paul, who was called by the exalted Lord. He is 'spirit and power'. He is present here and now among us. We can address him. At the same time he is also far above us. He is not only present, acting for us now — he is also the one who is coming.

4.   The earthly Christ and the exalted Christ are the same. He whose risen body bore the wounds of his suffering carries the whole of his personal history in himself. Christ is no longer lying

in the crib, a child, nor is he still hanging on the cross. But he is the one to whom this happened. Our task, then, is to look at the same time at the man who was and who is, to address him and to let him speak to us. Let us consider a few contrasting examples. The Christ who preached the Sermon on the Mount, whose feet were covered with the dust of the roads of Palestine, who caressed children and accepted the poor . . . is the same as the Christ who called Paul . . . who is now present in our community, speaks to us and is active among us . . . who will come and will consummate everything. In a word, we must have the whole Lord in mind.

5.   We grow towards an understanding of Christ's relationship with the Father, by observing what he did during his life on earth. He prayed constantly to the Father and continues this life of prayer in his glorification, living still 'to make intercession for us' (Heb 7. 25). His prayer for us enables us to share increasingly in his relationship with the Father and at the same time in his relationship with our fellow men. What he has experienced in this respect and is still experiencing will gradually become our experience as well. This brings us to the sixth and last direction.

6.   We share in Christ's life. What he accomplished on the cross — giving himself totally to God for us — is at the same time his permanent risen life. But even more, by giving us his Spirit, he has drawn us into this life of the resurrection. The last stage of Christian living is to share in the risen life of the Lord. We have the task of grasping this reality in our meditation and experiencing it at the deepest level. The more we do this, the more fully are we 'in Christ Jesus'. We know, however difficult this task may sometimes seem, that Christ himself wants this for us.

How are we to do this? On the one hand, we should have our Lord in mind as Paul did when he was converted — we should see him as Paul saw him or then or perhaps as he is depicted on the mosaics, enthroned, above the altars of early churches. On the other hand, we should also look into ourselves, where Christ has given us his Spirit and where that Spirit lives in us.

How often we meditate about one aspect of Christ, one word or one action in his life! This is always good, but we must also patiently try to grasp the whole of Christ, to penetrate to his unfathomable divine depths and appreciate as much as we can of his totality. The greatest task confronting every Christian is to know more and more of the 'unsearchable riches of Christ' (Eph 3. 9). He is to 'have life and have it abundantly' (Jn 10. 10) and to be one with him (Jn 17. 21-26). We should, then, devote our lives to this end and meditate about this mystery in a process that will last until our death.

14. The great events of salvation

Some important hints

It is not possible to provide material in a book of this kind which will lead to a celebration, in meditation, of all the events in the Church's year. It is, however, possible to give a number of hints which will point out ways in which some of the material that is already available in the great feasts especially can be used for meditation. In fact, it is precisely this available material which enables most Christians to meditate, particularly as a community of believers.

Let us consider some of these aspects of the Church's liturgy that help us to meditate. In the first place, the celebration of God's works of love and salvation — this can overwhelm us and renew our lives, especially if we have taken part in this celebration since we were children. The form which the celebration takes is also an aid to meditation — the saving events, communally celebrated, arouse and sustain our meditation. The whole liturgical celebration experienced externally and inwardly by the assembled people is a powerful incentive to group meditation. The liturgy is, moreover, celebrated in a cycle of recurring seasons, each representing one great aspect of our salvation in and through Christ — Advent and Christmas, Lent and Easter, culminating in the consummation of the death and resurrection of Christ and his sending of the Spirit at Pentecost. This seasonal presentation of the events of our salvation can lead us to great depths of meditation. Countless Christians have been caught up in a very deep experience of the presence of God in the course of these liturgical celebrations of the great saving events of the Church's year and, even though the word 'meditation' may not have occurred to them, they have indeed been led to meditate. We may say with conviction, then, that the Church's year is the great school for meditation which all Christians can attend.

How to meditate in the liturgy

Before taking part in the liturgical celebration, penetrate as deeply as possible into the heart of the mystery that is to be celebrated, perhaps by reading the text of the liturgy. Actively participating in the liturgy itself, allow the essential teaching of the feast celebrated to have its full effect on you. Afterwards, meditate about the experience of the communal celebration and the content of the liturgy. Let the thought of the event celebrated live on in you for as long as possible.

15. The 'We' in the liturgy – leading to meditation

The liturgy offers so much material for meditation that it is possible only to mention one or two aspects here, for example, the various signs, actions and gestures, the texts, the words of the texts themselves and, as a particular example, the word 'we', which plays a very important part in the liturgy. We will take this word and consider it now as a point of departure for meditation.

We must, in the first place, make this 'we' a living reality. 'We' are this elderly man, that young woman with her child, the young man over there – and me. We belong together. We are here for the same reason . . . We are all people and have a similar destiny . . . We are closely united in our aim . . . We must go forward together and overcome, each one of us, our captivity within ourselves and our separation from each other.

This reality, however, goes even deeper. Deeper than the assembly of people and deeper than each individual taking part in the liturgy, lies the mystery that we must try to reach – the mystery of Christ, the Lord. 'You are all one in Christ Jesus' (Gal 3. 28). Everything that is good in the other people present here and participating in the liturgy with me, is really the life of the Lord in this community. He has drawn all men to himself (Jn 12. 32). He pours his life into all men. He sums up everything in himself. In this community gathered together in this place to celebrate the presence of the Lord, we see the real mystery of the vine and the bread of life: 'He . . . abides in me and I in him' (Jn 6. 56). All those who are present are open to and seen by Christ.

This exercise is best carried out before the Eucharist (Holy Communion, or the Lord's Supper) on Sunday. It can be done very satisfactorily together with others. It can also be continued during the services. As it is repeated, it is possible to extend one's vision to include many different kinds of people — not only those who are present, but also those who are not there, professional people, the sick, the poor, children, young people, married and engaged couples, the old, the dying, those who are open and those who have become closed or hard, the isolated . . . We can extend our vision even further and include the Church throughout the world . . .

How to carry out this meditation

Many people will find the procedure outlined above sufficient for meditation. Others may prefer to carry out the meditation in a different way. One way is simply to contemplate the reality of this 'we' in the liturgy and let it penetrate as deeply as possible into one's innermost being. Another way is to go through a bowl movement, beginning with a simple perception of what is externally visible, continuing to a will to love and serve one's fellow men as a community and as individuals and finally going on to experience a unity with Christ and the beginning of an understanding of the mystery of Christ that embraces all things.

It may be that certain words or phrases arise in the course of this meditation — for example, 'we are in you', 'you are in him', 'he is in you', 'we are one in you' and so on. These words express the reality that has been grasped and at the same time lead to a firmer and deeper grasp. As soon as we have a glimpse of movement of the Spirit, we should plunge ourselves into it and let it carry us with Christ to God. The 'we' in the liturgy is always on the way towards God, in the words of the liturgy itself, 'through Christ, with him and in him'.

16. The source of love

The following exercise can be used over the years. The reality
with which it aims to bring us into contact can be grasped more and
more deeply as we continue to practise this meditation.

The material

1.   'God is love' (Jn 4. 8).
2.   God gave Jesus Christ to the world as a source of this love. In
every aspect of Jesus' earthly life, this love flows from him.
3.   Since his exaltation, Christ has not given even a spoonful of
soup to any poor person — apart from us. We are the channels
through which his love flows from the source into the world.
4.   As channels, we must be open to him, our source, so that
the water can flow in and we must also be open to the world, so
that the water can be given to our fellow men.

Ways to meditation

There are many different ways of meditating about this reality,
some of them mutually complementary. A selection can be made
from those suggested below.
1.   I settle down peacefully and in recollection. Then I let scenes
from the gospels arise within me. In these words and deeds of Jesus,
I recognize the pouring out of God's love. Jesus' healing of sick
people, his Sermon on the Mount, his going about with and talking
to the disciples, his death on the cross — all these show him as the
source of love for this world. I contemplate these scenes and remain
in them. I feel thankfulness or joy.
2.   I inwardly contemplate the exalted Christ. It is from him,
through his Spirit, that love enters men and thus comes into the
world. I think of the very many people in whom this love is present
and is expressed in words and deeds, in commitment to others, in
understanding and helping them, serving and counselling them and
in passing on the love of God to them in so many ways. I contemplate
the immense number of people from whom the love of Christ flows.
I am led from this to contemplate the source of love himself.
3.   I recall the many times that I have experienced selfless love in
my own life. I meditate about the reality of this love, which arose

in Christ and reached other people through people who are channels coming from this source . . .

4.   I open myself completely to this source – looking, listening, longing, receiving, thanking . . .

5.   I open myself completely to my fellow men, so that the love that urges me to live can flow out in my whole attitude and in everything that I do, in all my encounters with other people . . .

6.   It is impossible for me to be disappointed because the water comes from him, flows through me and thus reaches them. I reflect about this reality.

7.   How can we express this love? We can show it in our faces, our eyes, the palms of our hands, our mouths with a friendly, helpful word or good advice. Are there any other means of expressing it? This love that comes from Christ can be made tangible and visible in our very bodies . . . We are channels leading from the source that is Christ . . . a source which can never dry up . . .

8.   In serving others and expressing our love for them, we experience God's love flowing through us . . . This is the action of the Holy Spirit in us, the Spirit of Christ . . . the love of God flowing from this source . . . through us, the channel . . . to all appearances almost as a matter of course into the world . . .

9.   Later on, when these or some of the variations on this theme of the source of love and ourselves as channels of that love have been practised for some time and the idea has penetrated into our consciousness, we can continue with great simplicity and peace, sinking down into the depth of our own being – making use perhaps of the fundamental exercise to do this – until we reach the point where the life of Christ flows into us. Remain in this state, letting the flowing go on until it becomes complete. Then wait . . .

10.   Another way of meditating about this mystery is to let the 'water' of love flow from the source through your body into your hands and face . . . Let it flow to those parts of the body where this love can be expressed . . . to the hands and the face . . . Remain in contact with the source of love and the end of that love by doing things every day for others . . . let the water flow unceasingly . . . be a channel of God's love that refreshes and brings life to others.

17. Stages of love of your neighbour

It is always possible to meditate at a deep level about our simple actions and our fellow men. We can also meditate about our activities directed towards other people, about what happens between us and our fellow men and the way in which we express our love of our neighbour. Examples of this procedure are retrospective meditations, in which we consider, for instance, a past conversation, or forward-looking meditations, in which we anticipate an encounter that is to take place in the near future, and present meditations about what is happening here and now. What is most important, however, is that meditation must always be accompanied here by action. The action by which we express our love of our neighbour has its origin and inspiration in our meditation. The opposite is also true — our meditation is deeply affected by what we do and nourished by it.

Given below are twenty-six forms of love of our neighbour which may help to stimulate our meditation and our action. I provide no material leading to meditation, but leave this entirely to the reader, who will find that the meditative procedure will in fact be determined by his own attitude, that of the other person involved, the situation and the encounter. He may find a useful stimulus to meditation about the love of his neighbour in the sections on 'We' and the 'Source of love'. It is quite possible to extend meditation to include the Spirit, the life of Christ in other people with which we can come into contact through the Spirit. It is, however, difficult to say anything meaningful about this here without going against the inner laws of meditation.

The stages of love of our neighbour are: attentiveness to others — friendliness — openness — understanding — consideration — benevolence — giving way — recognition — helping — sharing — making friends — giving — caring — praying for others — serving — undertaking things for others — being there for others — making other people's interests one's own — making one's professional work an expression of love for others — reconciliation with others — declaring oneself to be at one with others — remaining at all times in an attitude of love — treating one's enemies as one's friends — showing mercy — magnanimity — total commitment.

18. The prayer of repetition

The prayer of repetition is a very simple and effective way of reaching the depths of meditation. This prayer very often arises from the deepest levels of consciousness and is therefore usually sincere, authentic and rich in content. Francis of Assisi, for example, prayed all night long on the mountain of La Verna the simple prayer 'My God and my all'.

These prayers express a certain maturity in faith. At the same time, because they are so simple, they can be used profitably by everyone, including children. They are said quietly again and again and usually inwardly. They help to bring one into a state of recollection and act as a guard against distraction. The inner life of the person who uses the prayer of repetition regularly and correctly will become deeper and more intense. The person praying will be changed and will become more closely united with God. This process is certainly possible in the case of a prayer said only once, but it takes place more naturally when the prayer of repetition is used.

There are clearly certain times then the prayer of repetition can be most easily practised – during quiet walks, when one is alone, at times during work of relaxation when one is unlikely to be disturbed, during the transition from reflection to meditation proper and finally at night when one is unable to sleep.

Here are a few examples of such prayers. The reader will be able to add suitable prayers of his own as his experience increases.

See, Lord, how poor I am.
Without you I am nothing (cf. Jn 15. 5).
I believe; help my unbelief (Mk 9. 24).
Thy will be done.
Praise be to you, Lord!
Take everything from me that prevents me from reaching you.
Make us ready for you!
Give me a love that is afraid of nothing.
Perfect your people in your love.
You overwhelm me with your love.
I remain in your silence.
Come, Holy Spirit!
You are all in all.

It is possible to repeat these prayers by fitting them into the rhythm of your bodily movements, for example, while you are walking, breathing or carrying out certain routine tasks.

19.　Getting up – an everyday action – a testimony

It was morning. I woke up. I sat up. I got up. Standing up, I was rising, rising again, resurrected. I paused to consider this. The external event was a sign of what was taking place within me. A deeper awakening and resurrection was felt within the external waking and getting up – the risen Christ was living in me and giving me a share in his life . . . I was living the life of resurrection . . . The one who had been resurrected and given new life and new power was living in me and expressing himself in my life . . .

I am, then, not simply awakened and resurrected in the purely biological and psychological sense. I am awakened and resurrected to a life lived from the central depth of all being which is the life of my own life . . .

Everything that I shall do today will be a sharing in his life. All my actions will be for his life, his praise, his love . . .

Resurrected to new life, I look forward to the day ahead. The future has already begun in me. I experience within myself the new life of obedience to Christ that God has brought about in me. I experience joy, power, trust, goodness, openness to others, love . .

Now I am truly human because I am in Christ. I am living at a truly human level and am truly myself. Everything that I do is a sign of his life and his activity in me. I live in Christ and he lives in me.

This is what took place in the morning. Throughout the whole day something of the freshness and vitality of this new beginning persisted and had its effect on all that I said and did.

20.　Hearing the word – conception and birth – leading to a meditation especially suitable for women

I hear a word – one of the Lord's words.

I let it penetrate into my innermost being and grow inside me.
It moves inside me, lives in me, changes me.
It wants to leave me, to enter the world, to be born.
I give birth to it in activity, in doing.
The word will in turn bring about life in the world.

As this exercise is repeated, the process can be taken to a deeper and deeper level — receiving the word of God, conceiving it, letting it sink down into the centre and the depth of one's being, letting it grow and become mature at this deep level and finally letting its urge to be born and present in the world be fulfilled. This whole process can be carried out through the medium of many different words or scriptural passages. Finally, we can take Mary as our example here, as she conceived the eternal Word and gave birth to it so that it could be heard in the world.

21. From without to within — a text to be read aloud and repeated frequently

I sit in a quiet room. The door is closed. On the door is a notice to say that I am not to be disturbed. The room surrounds me . . . encloses me . . . protects me and ensures that there will be no disturbances or interruptions . . . There are sounds outside, but they are a long way away . . . They do not reach me . . . I hear the quietness of the room . . .

My body is quite motionless. My feet and legs are drawn up . . . close to my body. The outer edges of my feet are resting on the ground . . . The upper parts of my legs are quite relaxed . . . I sit and feel how peaceful it is to sit here . . .

My forearms are drawn up and my wrists are lying on my calves. My hands are together, forming a bowl . . . I feel how open and receptive they are . . . They express externally my inner receptivity . . . I am ready to receive . . .

My body is straight but I have let it sink down into the pelvis so that it is resting there . . . My shoulders and the upper parts of my arms are quite relaxed . . . I continue the upright attitude of my body into my neck and the back of my head. This posture makes me fresh and relaxed . . . alert and ready . . . I feel this intensely . . .

I perceive the whole of my body and am aware of my attitude . . . as a whole and in the different parts of my body . . . I am conscious of what is expressed by my body — peace and recollectedness . . . an alert readiness . . . I persist in this attitude . . .

One movement continues to make itself felt   — my breathing. I am not actively breathing — I simply let it happen . . . and experience it . . . I direct it downwards as far downwards as possible . . . My ribs remain motionless . . . The movement of my breathing is only present around my waist . . .

Gradually I sink down inwardly with my breath . . . I sink down into my centre of gravity . . . into the lower part of my body . . . into my inner being . . . into the ground of my being . . . I let go of myself . . . relax completely . . . sinking lower and lower . . . I remain there, in the depth of my being.

The Spirit of Christ is given to me. Gradually I reach that Spirit . . . New, pure life comes to me from the exalted Christ . . . Everything that was in Christ is now in the Spirit . . . The Spirit is life of his life . . . I long for this life . . .

The life of the Lord is total surrender to the Father . . . in thanksgiving, praise, obedience and love . . . it is being present for others . . . for everyone in every situation . . . All this comes to me now . . . is offered to me . . . pours into me . . .

I am completely at rest . . . A prayer comes to me: 'glorify the Father in me' . . . I repeat it . . . again and again . . . I feel able to accept this perfectly . . . to let it take place within me . . . to participate in it . . . I offer myself to God . . . make myself available to him as a place where he can live . . . where the Father can be glorified . . . I remain in this for a long time . . .

You should always end this exercise by meditating quietly in full consciousness of your bodily position. Other prayers or variations on the concluding prayer 'glorify the Father in me' may suggest themselves to you at the end of the exercise. Expressed in simple words, they might take the following form: 'Glorify the Father through me', '. . . through us', 'Let me make your total self-surrender totally my own' and so on. We may also think of how God can use us to serve our fellow men and express this idea as a simple prayer: 'You are in me for all men', 'Act in me for them' or 'I ask you to be in me for them'. An even simpler prayer would be the one word

'You' —this is in itself pregnant with meaning. The same word can be used in prayer in a variety of simple contexts: 'I look for you', 'I love you', 'I honour you' etc.

22. Inner images and procedures — texts leading to meditation and to be read aloud

The following six meditations form a group on their own. A natural object is considered, meditated about at depth and allowed to act as a symbol. This may even lead to Christian meditation at a deep level. The more frequently these meditations are repeated, the more clearly will the reality underlying the image be seen. The intention, of course, is that the image should gradually recede and the reality to which it points should slowly emerge and come to the foreground.

These texts should only be read aloud when those present have reached the right level of maturity in the practice of meditation and the person who is reading has made the text completely his own and can therefore read it as an expression of what is taking place in his innermost being.

(a)   The inner abyss

The image of the inner abyss may be a great help in the practice of sinking down to one's inner depth. It is moreover an idea which often suggests itself to us quite spontaneously. Finally, it has proved itself to be helpful to many people even when it is constantly repeated.

This image of the inner abyss points to the immeasurable depths that are present in each of us. As in the case of all these meditations based on images, our aim should be to penetrate to the underlying reality in the course of the exercise.

We begin with the fundamental exercise. We take up the correct position for meditation. We breathe freely and rhythmically. As we breathe out we say or think: let go . . . sink down . . . sink into our own depth . . .

Sinking down, we recognize how deep this inner depth is. It is immeasurable. It is like an abyss and we stand at the top, looking over the edge between the two faces of rock, gazing down. In the rock a few little trees are growing, moss and tufts of grass... Slowly we sink down in this abyss . . . deeper and deeper . . . It is not dark . . . We sink down, deeper and deeper . . . We look down . . . Does it go as far as that place there? No that is not the bottom . . . New depths reveal themselves to our eyes . . . Further and further down it sinks . . .

Far below I see a strip of cloud floating . . . What does it mean? An image of the Spirit of God in me . . . quite silent . . . I sink down lower . . . I am received into the cloud . . . It envelops me . . . The sinking slows down . . . and ceases altogether . . . I do nothing. I remain there, in the abyss . . . I am received into the depth . . . remain in it . . . Let myself sink even lower . . .

I am in the depth of the ultimate reality, completely relaxed and completely trusting . . . I surrender myself completely . . . I float there, doing nothing, in the depth . . . I am very close to a mystery that is inexpressible . . . I expect nothing . . . I remain in this reality.

(b)   The inner tree

We look at a tree, take it into our innermost self and observe, after a little while, how closely we are in accordance with this inner tree. We are identical with the tree. It is a symbol of our own being and helps us to sink deeper into that being. A further stage may then take place — we enter the ultimate mystery and our life becomes more real because of it.

We sit in an attitude of recollection, breathing freely — letting go and sinking down into meditation, so that we are led, by the regular and peaceful rhythm of our breathing, into an even deeper state of peace. Closing our eyes, we persist in this state, motionless.

We imagine that we are walking in the country through fields and woods . . . We leave the world and enter a large field, in the middle of which is a great tree. We look at this tree . . . We see how its roots grip into the ground . . . We contemplate the massive trunk rising up out of the soil, so thick that even ten men could not destroy it . . . We look at the point where the branches begin to grow out of the stem . . . and the great rounded top with the many twigs and leaves growing from them . . . The whole crown of the tree is covered with broad green leaves . . . We contemplate this great, noble tree peacefully and let its powerful shape have its effect on us . . . The tree is in itself comforting. We let its being enter us . . . We contemplate it and breathe it in . . . It enters us more and more fully . . . until it has penetrated into our innermost being.

The tree's roots penetrate into our being, growing deeper and deeper into us . . . they spread out inside us . . .

Above the roots the powerful trunk rises up inside me . . . Slowly it grows up towards my heart . . . It gives me strength, constancy, uprightness . . . I let this great, sturdy trunk bear me up and give me support . . . I draw nourishment from it . . . I am this trunk . . .

Above the trunk the great branches spread out inside me . . . From the branches grow the twigs . . . on all sides . . . I spread out . . . give myself the freedom to grow and develop, spreading out in to the air around me . . . Leaves grow out, too many to count . . . They breathe the air that surrounds me . . . and live from it . . . They are fed by the light that comes from above . . . I experience all this and feel how good this life is.

In this way, I stand, strong yet supple, in myself . . . deeply rooted in the ground of my being . . . powerfully supported by my trunk . . . growing out into countless twigs and leaves . . . rising up . . . into the world . . . spreading out around me on all sides . . . and yet held together as one being in me . . . I experience this being . . . I experience it as deeply as possible . . . I am conscious of my existence . . . I am given to myself . . . I am given up to myself.

Standing like this in myself, in fulness of being, I am aware of my roots and where they are — in the ultimate ground of my being, of all being . . . I am aware of the branches and twigs — they grow out into the freedom of the air that surrounds me, into the free space of my existence, of all existence and into the mystery of that existence . . . My whole being is growing up, reaching up as high as possible . . . It is given light, the ultimate light of all being. My being flourishes in that light and bears fruit . . . This fruit is there for the happiness of others . . . and for the honour and glory of the ultimate, invisible reality from which everything proceeds and to which everything is directed . . . I am rooted . . . surrounded . . . spread out . . . given . . . I flourish and bear fruit . . . My being reaches out to the ultimate mystery that sustains and nourishes me and gives me life . . .

(c)   *The inner cross*

In this exercise, we let a cross form itself within us. We begin at the centre of this cross. This is at the level of our heart at the very centre of our body. We let the wood of the cross grow slowly inside us. From deep down within us life rises up. This can be seen in the image of the rising bubbles.

At the level of my heart I feel my breast bone at the very centre of my body. Within me I see the point at which two lines cross. Nothing else . . .

Very slowly one of these lines – the vertical post of the cross – grows from this central point downwards. It reaches my waist, crosses it and continues to move down . . . lower and lower until it reaches the very ground of my being . . . There it stays, firmly embedded . . . It gives me great strength. I am conscious of that strength.

Now I see small silver bubbles rising up out of the ground in which the vertical wood of the cross is fixed. These are symbols of the life of holiness given to me by Christ. They float up, encircling the wood, up and up, filling me with new life . . .

Now the bubbles have reached the point where the horizontal beam crosses the vertical post. The bubbles continue to rise through my body into my head and, as they rise, so the post grows upwards with them as far as the crown of my head. I feel this post supporting me from the top of my head down to the ground of my being. Very slowly I follow the line of the post down . . . then up again.

I feel the line within me from the lowest to the highest point of my body as the bubbles rise. These points are kept apart, but at the same time they are united . . . I am conscious of this . . .

There is a movement upwards in this vertical line of the cross – praise of God and a total surrender to him . . . I am borne up by the life of Christ . . . There is also a movement downwards – from top to bottom, down into my depths . . .

After a little while, I go to the central point. Slowly, from the centre, two lines grow out, to the right and to the left . . . This horizontal beam, moving in opposite directions, reaches my shoulders . . . moves into my arms, towards my hands . . . going towards the people who surround me . . .

This slow movement which begins at the central point of the cross is a movement from Christ himself, at the centre of my life. Life goes from that centre . . . I let the cross stand quietly in me. It bears me up . . . It gives me strength . . . The bubbles are now moving along the horizontal beam of the cross in both directions . . . Everything is filled with the life of Christ . . . The movement of Christ's life is everywhere . . . I do nothing . . . I just remain conscious of the powerful effect that this image is having in me . . . It gives me support, direction and strength . . .

(d) The inner bowl

If we have a bowl with a good, simple shape, we can place it in front of us on an empty table covered with a plain cloth. Let this bowl have its effect and sink into meditation. Alternatively, we can shut our eyes and let the image of a bowl present itself. It is not a difficult shape to imagine. What is important is to decide which of the two courses to take before beginning to meditate.

I take up the position for meditation. I sink down into peace . . . Peace fills me . . . I breathe freely and rhythmically . . . As I breathe I am conscious of the words of the fundamental exercise — let go . . . sink down . . . I am quite peaceful and recollected . . .

In front of me I see a beautiful bowl. It is firm and motionless . . . It reaches outwards and upwards . . . It is quite ready . . . ready to receive . . . Nothing can prevent it receiving . . . It is pure receptiveness . . .

I am deeply affected by this essential characteristic of the bowl — its receptiveness. The bowl has something, is something that I am not or that I do not yet have . . . It is possible that it may have something to give me, something that will make me richer, something that will make me whole . . . The essence of the bowl should be my essence. It should enter my being . . .

I look at the bowl in front of me and breathe it in . . . It penetrates deeper and deeper into my being . . . Soon it is within me . . . in the lower part of my body . . . I feel it resting there . . . I see it inside me . . . It is empty . . . Its wall is very thin . . . Most of it is empty space . . . nothing . . . emptiness . . . It is quite open . . . When flowers, for example, are put in it, it disappears even more

. . . it is only there for what it contains. . .

The bowl that is in me represents something of my own being
. . . It arouses something in me . . . The bowl is receptive . . . What
must I be open to receive? I should surely be quite open to everything, resisting nothing . . . I persist in this total receptiveness.
I wait . . . I am aware that I am given in some way something valuable.

After a little while, the bowl reveals something else of its essence
to me. It preserves. It encloses what is entrusted to it . . . Silently,
patiently and faithfully . . . Its wall is high, but open . . . like out-
stretched arms . . It is there to receive and to preserve . . . It does
not look out for anything new, but simply preserves what it is given
. . . Silently, it serves and preserves . . .

Finally, I realize what the bowl offers . . . It offers us what it
contains . . . It is entirely giving and giving away . . . Should I not
offer everything, give everything, give myself away? I should become
a bowl . . .

I contemplate the bowl in me. It belongs to me. It represents my
essential being . . . I leave it there, inside me. I become a bowl more
and more . . . my whole being is bowl-like — receiving, preserving,
offering . . . I persist in this contemplation of the bowl . . . considering the image of the bowl and becoming myself bowl-like.

(e)   Inner water

The material provided below for this exercise may be used, but it
should be remembered that it is only one way of exploiting the
image of water in meditation.

The material

'My soul thirsts for thee; . . . as in a dry and weary land where no
water is' (Ps 63. 1). These words of the psalmist express an inner
experience in which I too can share. His inner life, he is saying, is
like dry earth, hardened, infertile and dead. This image goes together
with the words of the evangelist which anticipate the experience of
the future: 'If you knew the gift of God and who it is that is saying
to you "Give me a drink", you would have asked him, and he would
have given you living water' (Jn 4. 10).

This promise can be compared with another promise in the same
Gospel: 'If anyone thirst, let him come to me and drink. He who

believes in me, as the scripture has said, "Out of his heart shall flow rivers of living water" ' (Jn 7. 38). The author provides the interpretation of this in the words that follow: 'Now he said this about the Spirit, which those who believed in him were to receive' (Jn 7. 39).

This promise is fulfilled and has become our experience. We pray now in the sequence at Pentecost: 'On our dryness pour thy dew'. The land that is within us should be saturated with this water and be made soft, living and fertile. I would like to experience this myself.

The meditation

I sit, breathing rhythmically, completely relaxed, silent, present and quite at peace.

In the ground of my being, I am conscious of the dry land. The soil is hardened and cracked. There is no vegetation. Even the moss is dried up.

At the deepest level of my being, there is water. It rises up very slowly, at first just filtering through to the roots . . . They absorb the water that gives them life . . . The earth in me offers itself to the water . . . Allows it to penetrate . . . The water sinks in, making everything fertile . . . It refreshes the roots of my being . . . I begin to recover . . .

I let this water enter me. Thirsting, languishing, I long for it . . . I offer myself, my innermost being, to this life-giving water. I give complete freedom to this water that is coming into me . . . open all my pores to it so that it can enter me at every point . . . I surrender myself without reserve to this water . . . I become conscious of it as a life-giving force, something that can change me . . . I expose myself totally to this transformation which will result in my becoming totally myself . . . and in which nothing will be lost . . . and I will become conscious of my true being . . . and will achieve perfect freedom . . . All I have to do to receive this water is to relax, breathe freely, persist . . . remain open . . . be there . . . present . . . and let myself be changed and given . . .

At the end of this meditation, I thank God for the gift of his Spirit, ask him to forgive me for having been inattentive and pray: 'Send forth thy Spirit and they are created; and thou renewest the face of the ground' (Ps 104. 30).

(f)   Silence in silence

I sit in the position for meditation. I am alone. My door is closed
and my room is very quiet. Peace encloses me. The sounds outside
are a long way away. I listen to the peace of the room . . . In my
innermost self I am as quiet as a lake when there is no wind . . .
clear and motionless . . . a still lake in the forest . . .

I am silent. I share in the silence of nature . . . the silence of the
roots of the trees . . . of the grass . . . of the depths of the lake . . .
I share in the silence of the land, the sea, the stars . . . of the universe
. . . I share in the silence of God . . .

The silence within me is becoming deeper and deeper. I sink
down into the sphere of wordless silence . . . into the sphere of
God's silence . . . In his silence there is fulness . . . and he is entirely
present . . . There is no need for words . . . He is completely in this
silence . . . I let myself enter the silence of God . . .

It is a silence without end . . . fathomless . . . a deep abyss of
silence . . . and I am in it, quite at peace . . . in God's fulness . . .
a fulness that contains everything . . .

I wait . . . I breathe . . . without moving . . . With my silence I
am in your silence . . . I have no intention at all . . .

Your silence penetrates into my innermost being . . . I am silent
in your silence . . . Your silence is silent in me . . . This is silence
in silence . . . There is nothing else.

23. 'You' – addressed by and addressing Christ – a text for guidance, leading to meditation

When I address Christ, I often use the word 'you' in a superficial
way. My intention is sincere enough, but I am not fully present and
do not commit myself fully. I do not put myself entirely into that
'you'.

So now I become quite still and recollected. I breathe deeply and
steadily, letting go and sinking down into the depth of my being.
I stay there. The word 'You' comes to me. Does it come from me?
Or does it come from him?

1. *The 'you' that comes from the exalted Christ*

(a) This word 'You' comes from above – from him.
He utters this word . ... I hear it inside me . . . I am addressed by him . . . He addresses me with the word 'you' . . .

(b) The word 'You' pierces me like a ray of light.
It comes down, from above, through my head . . . through my knowledge . . . my experience . . . my will . . . Deeper and deeper it penetrates . . . through my breast . . . passing through my heart . . . going deeper and deeper into the ground of my being . . . Everything in me is lit up by this word 'you' . . . It makes everything in me transparent . . . My whole being shines . . . I am fully recognized and fully accepted . . .

(c) He calls me when he calls me 'you'.
My whole being begins to awaken when he calls me 'you' . . . I am called to life by the word . . . I become alert to him . . . open to him . . . ready to receive him . . . He calls me . . . Hearing him call me, I let myself be filled with him . . . In this word 'you', he flows into me and I come to life for him and respond to his call . . .

2. *My response to him*

(a) From my innermost depth the word 'You' rises up.
From the ground of my being I respond to Christ. I answer his 'you' to me and call him 'You' . . . the word rises in me and moves to him . . .

(b) How much this word 'You' embraces!
Calling him 'You' I am addressing the whole Christ – my lord and master . . . the crucified Christ . . . the glorified, exalted Christ . . . my brother and my Lord . . . Again and again I try to embrace the whole Lord with this word 'You' . . . to penetrate him entirely . . . to grasp his fulness and truth . . . I meditate about this for as long as possible . . .

When this meditation is repeated – and it bears repetition – it may be useful to think of the following aspects of the word 'you'. Firstly, we call each other 'you' and this implies an openness to others, an intimacy and a depth in our relationship with them. Secondly, there are many striking examples of the use of this word in the Bible. It is worth reflecting about the statement in Isaiah:

'I have called you by your name, you are mine' (Is 43. 1), the evangelist's 'And Jesus looking upon him loved him and said to him . . .' (Mk 10. 21) and Paul's words to Jesus: 'Who are you, Lord?' (Acts 9. 5).

Finally, this meditation is particularly suitable after holy communion.

24. The total mystery in the individual thing – leading to meditation

There are many individual things in the world which are very beautiful, moving, or inspiring. Spend a little time thinking about those aspects of creation that have been especially meaningful to you – anything that you have found precious, lovely or powerful or that has astonished you, made you very happy, fulfilled you or given you a sense of liberation.

All these individual things bear traces of the one who created them, and something of the beauty of the creator breaks through in each of them, like sunlight shining through a pane of frosted glass.

In this exercise, we shall try to experience the way in which the underlying total mystery of the creator breaks through in the individual things that move us powerfully.

The individual thing	*The experience*	*The total mystery*
A house	Security	'Under his wings you will find refuge' (Ps 91. 4)
Bread	Satisfaction	The only one who in the end satisfies us (Ps 91.16)
Ripe fruit	A pleasant taste	The ultimate delight and sweetness (see Ps 16. 1; 36. 9)
A rose	Beauty	The fulness and beauty of the ultimate mystery (see Ps 50. 2)
Driving on a motorway	Being constantly given and fulfilled	The all-embracing gift and immeasurable fulfilment (see Ps 107. 9)
A symphony	The fulness	Ultimate fulfilment and

concert	and unity of life	unity (see Jn 1. 16; Col. 2. 9)
A book containing deep thoughts	Depth and wisdom	'As the heavens are higher than the earth . . . so are my thoughts higher than your thoughts' (Is 55. 9) 'O the depth of . . . the wisdom of God' (Rom 11. 33)
In a circle of friends, one person understands me	I am understood	The one who understands me completely and knows my deepest being (see Ps 138. 1-4)
Someone supports and encourages me	I transcend myself and thus become fully myself	The one who is able to release me from bitterness and defeat and leads me on to fulness of life (see Jn 10. 10)
Someone helps me when I am in trouble I am not left in the lurch	Trust and reliability	'I will be with him in in trouble' (Ps 91.15) 'My rock' (Ps 28. 1) 'Thou . . . my help' (Ps 27. 9)
A sign of tenderness	The tenderness of love	The love which loves in every dimension of love (see Jn 4. 8)

There are many individual things of this kind, apart from those given above — the sun, the snow, a spring of water, fire, wind, a bird's nest, a car, the roof of a house, a melody, a meal, the conversation of friends, marriage, forgiveness, being loved. Every good things and every good encounter with another person can lead to an insight into the ultimate mystery. The total mystery is revealed in our encounter with all these small, individual aspects of creation. We are given, we are consoled and we are illuminated by the total mystery of God. All that we have to do is to be consciously looking for that mystery. We may well pray with the Church, therefore, asking God to pour his love into our hearts so that we may love him in everything and above everything, and, with Ignatius of Loyola, love God in everything. Finally, we recall the words 'Heaven and earth are full of his glory'.

Meditating about this mystery

Many people may want the subject to be developed a little more; they may want to know what is the most suitable time for meditating about these individual things and what is the most suitable place. They may also feel a need for more detailed help.

The best time for meditation is undoubtedly during or immediately after experiencing the thing in question — seeing the rose, hearing the concert, reading the book and so on. The most suitable place would clearly be a quiet spot on the edge of a forest, in the garden or any place indoors, preferably with a good view from the window. After reaching a deep level of experience in the fundamental exercise, let yourself remain in a relaxed, peaceful and recollected attitude in the presence of the thing that has moved or inspired you. It may then be given to you — you may receive, for example, its beauty, fulness, strength, tenderness or whatever else it has to offer you and you may then be permitted to go beyond this to the total mystery behind it and be granted an insight into the 'all in all' of that mystery.

Finally, certain prayers may suggest themselves to you in the course of this meditation and these may well be of the type that can be frequently repeated. Examples of this kind of prayer are: 'You are all in all' or 'You are my God and my all'.

25. Growing old in hope — leading to meditation

1.   I am becoming older. Slowly but certainly I am losing everything that I used to have. (Think about this gradual loss with increasing years in detail — the loss of youthful energy and health, youthful good looks and freshness, earlier friendships that were so easy to form, the possibilities that were open to you when you were younger, your status and your position in society . . . even the loss of your teeth or hair . . .) I have to let these things go . . . I must not think that I can keep them . . .

2.   What has become of everything that I have lost? It is not simply lost. I have lost it, but God has gathered it up ... to use for his own intentions ... for me ... I have let it go, but not for ever ... God is keeping it for me and he will go on doing that so long as I give it to him ...

3.   God will complete and fulfil all that I have lost. When I die, he will gather me up as well ... Then he will bring together all that I have lost and make everything new. 'Behold, I make all things new' (Rev 21. 5). He will give it all back to me, complete it and fulfil it, complete and fulfil me ... He will complete and fulfil all of us ... the whole world ... everything.

4.   Full of trust, I let everything go. I give him everything, in hope, expecting the fulfilment of all things. I give it to him as I give money to the savings bank ... I am ready to do without, so that he can carry out his intentions ... I entrust everything to his keeping ... He will complete, renew and fulfil everything ...

26. 'Behold, I make all things new' — leading to meditation

The text

Everything in my experience that is good is really a gift to me — the morning and the evening are gifts, the tree that I see and the bread that I eat, being understood and being reconciled. All these are gifts, but, like every human experience, they are limited. Because of their limitations, they cannot ultimately satisfy me. They are also incomplete and defective.

Let us, then, think about the words: 'Behold, I make all things new' (Rev 21. 5).

What does this mean, this promise that everything will be changed and renewed? It means in the first place that God will make all things new, whole and complete. He will bring together everything that is broken or isolated. He will restore health to the sick. 'He will wipe away every tear ... and death shall be no more, neither shall there be mourning nor crying nor pain any more, for the former things have passed away' (Rev 21. 4).

This renewal of all things, however, goes even deeper. God,

according to St Paul, is 'all in all'. In other words, in every individual thing there is something of the all-embracing, total mystery of God himself — God who is all. What is more, God is in a sense already, even now, present 'all in all'. This means that each individual good thing will be the place where the totality of goodness will appear. God will be the all in all things, not something that is present. In every individual thing in his creation, he will let the fulness of his goodness break through. He will overcome all the limitations of all individual things — and all individual beings — and let the all-embracing totality of goodness become apparent.

The meditation

Many people will find that the very idea of God making all things new will automatically cause astonishment, joy and expectation. These people can remain peacefully considering this theme and experiencing at the deepest possible level what it means to them.

Others will prefer to go on to meditation in a series of steps. They may, for instance, find it useful to apply what is said above, in the text, to individual experiences, perhaps even unhappy ones, or to people who, by their faults or difficult attitudes, have caused them suffering. Some readers, who find the fulness of Christian faith difficult, may even prefer to begin with different material altogether.

27. Adoration — leading to meditation

There are three steps to adoration — unlimited admiration, unconditional subjection and joyful self-surrender.

It is not too difficult to summarize each of these steps in a simple word or group of words which can be repeated. In this way, you will gradually sink down into the depths of meditation and adoration.

Unlimited admiration — you might, for example, repeat the words 'How great you are!' or 'How incomprehensible you are!' or 'Your mystery is beyond my reach!'.

Unconditional subjection — 'Here I am, Lord!' or 'Do what you like with me' or 'Take me and use me'.

Joyful self-surrender — 'You are an unfathomable ocean of love' or 'Make a joyful noise to the Lord, all the lands' (Ps 100. 1) or 'I desire nothing but you' or 'My God and my all'.

It may happen that these words will lead you directly to adoration. This is even more likely to take place if you bear in mind God's glory and the immeasurable fulness of his love and if this thought inflames your heart and makes you glow in the depths of your being.

28. Taking the fundamental exercise to a deeper level

Anyone who practises the fundamental exercise for a long time will certainly acquire a deeply meditative attitude. At the same time, however, he will inevitably begin to ask, at some stage or other, how he ought to continue with this important and indispensable exercise. Each of the individual statements — let go, sink down, become one, let come (or become new) — can be taken to a much deeper level that one might at first imagine. However, it might also prove useful to continue along the following lines.

Treat each of the following fourteen sections as an exercise lasting for one day. If you feel that you cannot spend so much time as this on each exercise, just carry out the exercises as you come to them without troubling too much about the time they take. Beginners may find the first exercise the most suitable.

1. *I sink into silence*

I am far removed from all noise. I have no intention. I have no thoughts. I want nothing . . . It is becoming quieter and quieter . . . I sink deeper and deeper . . . I continue in silence . . . in deep silence . . . It is becoming emptier and emptier . . . But this emptiness is not a nothingness . . . Another, deeper and greater reality makes itself felt . . .

2. *I sink into the depths*

Into my depth . . . the depths of my own being, which is fathomless . . . I let myself go more and more and sink deeper and deeper . . . An unsuspected depth is revealed . . . I remain in this depth . . . far removed from the surface of my everyday life . . . far below my everyday consciousness . . .

3.   *I let go and come to myself*

I let go of myself more and more . . . let go of my narrow, faulty and self-seeking self . . . As I do so, I come more and more to myself . . . I become more and more free in the ground of my being . . . My essential dynamism is released more and more fully . . . that dynamic energy within me that is always tending towards the ultimate reality in which everything is gathered up and united . . . I sink deeper and deeper into this ground . . . into my real self . . . into the truth of myself . . . into my authentic self . . .

I become truly free . . . released . . . inwardly peaceful and united with myself . . . I become as I was intended to become.

4.   *I let go of everything that prevents the ground of my being from coming to life*

I let go of everything in me that is not authentic . . . everything that I have learnt or have been trained to do, in childhood or later in life, that is wrong . . . everything that forms an obstacle to my becoming what I was originally intended to become . . .

I allow what is present in the ground of my being to have its effect on me . . . to illuminate my entire being and to heal me . . . to make me whole . . . to inspire me . . . to fashion me . . . without any effort on my part to bring about an essential unity between all levels of my being . . .

At the same time, I become conscious, in the depth of my being, of a tendency within me towards the ultimate reality which contains all individual things and beings . . . from which my being comes . . . the reality that alone can satisfy me . . .

5.   *The more fully I let go, the more strongly I become conscious of this tendency within me*

This tendency in the depth of my being towards the ultimate reality is gradual and hidden, but at the same time so powerful that I cannot resist it . . . A tendency towards the ultimate, lasting and absolute reality . . . going beyond all individual beings and aspects of creation and in the direction of the reality that unites all these within itself . . . I am conscious of the depth of this ultimate experience . . . of its endless depth and fulness . . . It is the mystery of the God who is present but hidden . . .

6. *The ground of my being is borne up*

Like my body, which is borne up as I stand or sit . . . my innermost being is resting . . . borne up . . . It is not completely independent . . . I rest, in the ground of my being, on the ultimate ground of all being . . . In my being this ultimate being shines through . . . I let myself go . . . I sink down . . . My innermost being becomes one with the ultimate ground of all being . . . In this way I share in its absolute power . . .

7. *The ground of my being has entered the absolute ground of all being*

It is borne up and surrounded by the ultimate mystery . . . The lowest vault of my being rests on the ground of all being . . . The Spirit of God has entered me and dwells in me (see Rom 5. 5) . . . God is present and active in me . . .

The Spirit of God fills the depths of my being . . . sets me free from oppression, rigidity and death . . . helps to release my inner tendency towards the ultimate mystery . . . and to come, in the depth of my innermost being, to freedom, life and pure self-expression . . . The Spirit of God helps me to find my true form and expression . . . 'I will put a new spirit within them' (Ezek 11. 19) . . 'You have received the spirit of sonship' (Rom 8. 15).

8. *I let myself go completely and nothing is left in me to resist the activity of God*

The Spirit of God penetrates more and more deeply into my being the more fully I let go of myself and my limitations . . . the more fully I open myself to receive him . . . He is looking for me . . . seeking me out . . . seeking out the deepest recesses of my being . . . All I have to do is to let go of myself and let him come . . .

In letting go, I give myself to him . . . like a sick person giving himself in complete trust to the care of the doctor . . . I open myself to come, let my mask go and stand before him exactly as I am, unprotected . . . I remain quite still and let his Spirit pour into me . . . I am relaxed, but quite awake . . . I am ready to receive him . . .

9.   *I sink down towards the Spirit of God*

I plunge into the depth of this experience in the knowledge that I
will find him there . . . I let myself go . . . I sink down . . . deeply
into the Spirit of God . . . There I find life . . . the life of Christ . . .
the life that transforms me . . . so that I am 'conformed to the image
of the Son' (Rom 8. 29) . . . I let go . . . sink down . . . and become
one with this Spirit . . . the Spirit that fills me entirely.

10.   *'God has sent the Spirit of his Son into our hearts' (Gal 4. 6)*

In the first place, receiving this Spirit means that we receive the
attitude of Christ . . . accepting Christ as Lord in our lives . . . But
in the second place it also means that Christ is present in us and
active in a very special way: 'The Lord is the Spirit' (2 Cor 3. 17) . . .
Christ is the Spirit and he is present in me . . . I have the life of
Christ in me . . . his love, his obedience to the Father, his attitude of
adoration and his fellowship . . .

I let go . . . I sink down . . . I become one with the attitude of
Christ . . . with his life . . . with his Spirit in me . . . I let myself live
from Christ . . . My life will in this way become as mature as that of
Paul, when he wrote: 'It is no longer I who live, but Christ who
lives in me' (Gal 2. 20) . . . This life of Christ in me is unfathomable.

11.   *I die and become new*

The little, self-seeking, presumptuous and limited I dies . . . The
much greater and selfless I, full of the life of Christ, comes . . . I am
changed . . . transformed . . . made completely new . . . I die and
become new . . . This death is in no way terrifying . . . It is like
sickness dying into health or night dying into day . . . I die into a
new life.

12.   *I die and rise again*

In this, I am in touch with the central event of world history —
Christ's death and resurrection. I die with Christ . . . and share in
his resurrection . . . I meditate about this experience that takes place
in the centre and the depth of my being . . . With Paul, I die with
Christ . . . and live with him (Rom 6. 8; see also 8. 9; 8. 14-15).

13. *I am in Christ*

'He . . . abides in me and I in him' (Jn 6. 56). My task is to grow
more and more into him . . . He is like a coat that is too big for me
and I have to grow into it . . . I must develop in every way in order
to fit into it. 'You have put on Christ' (Gal 3. 27) — I now understand what this means. I am in him . . . 'We are to grow in every way
into him' (Eph 4. 15).

14. *He is in me*

Through his Spirit. He grows into me . . . He wants to be the life of
my life . . . I let myself be taken over by him . . . I give him complete
freedom . . . I become one with him . . . I remain in this experience
. . . I am supremely grateful . . . receptive . . . open . . .

29. Breathing as the symbol of our relationship with God — steps into deep meditation

The following text provides material for meditation in a series of
steps, which could take several months or even years. The whole
process is given below in a very condensed form. The later steps
presuppose a certain degree of maturity in meditation and beginners may find it easier to confine themselves to the earlier steps or,
if they attempt the later ones, to follow them in a fairly external or
analogous way.

It is advisable to spend as much time as possible at each stage and
in this way to carry it out as fundamentally as possible. It is also
worth returning to an earlier stage after a fairly long interval. You
will almost certainly find that your intervening experience in meditation will add to your appreciation of this stage when you go
through it again.

Each of the twelve paragraphs that follow is intended to provide
one exercise, sufficient for one day. It is better to keep to this
plan.

1.   I breathe. I know that I am breathing. I experience my breathing . . . (pause for as long as possible here). I try to watch while I
am breathing, without changing the rhythm. I stay watching . . .

2.   Breathing in, I know that I am being given . . . I can always breathe in air. The air is there. It is there for me . . .

3.   Breathing out, I experience deep relaxation . . . I am relaxed . . . I give back . . . I empty myself . . . I stay with this experience and try to penetrate as deeply as possible into its mystery . . .

4.   Thinking about my breathing, observing my breathing in and out, feeling its rhythm, I reflect about God . . . He is looking at me with love. The whole process of breathing comes from him. It is part of his process of creation . . . It is his gift to me . . . I receive it from him . . . I give up all tension . . . I give it to him . . .

6.   Breathing gives me refreshment, strength and new life. It is a constant source of life . . . As I breathe, new life pours into me and fills me . . . I live again . . .

6.   Breathing in, being given, God's looking at me — these are all signs of his love for me . . . I know that he loves me . . . Love seeks to penetrate every recess of my being and to fill me . . . Breathing is the symbol of God's love. As I breathe in, God's love breathes into me . . .

7.   Breathing out is also an expression of love. Love gives itself, gives itself away, pours itself out for others . . . Breathing out is a symbol of love . . . It is the sign of the love that comes from the centre of my being and flows out, giving itself . . . to him . . . into him . . . I stay for as long as possible meditating about breathing as a symbol of love . . . Two prayers occur to me and I say them as I breathe and meditate — you come to me . . . I go to you . . .

8.   Breathing becomes more and more real to me . . . It expresses a hidden reality, made tangible in the symbol of breathing . . . God really sends his breath, his love, his Holy Spirit to me . . . and this penetrates into my innermost being . . . and I am made a child of God . . . God's breath enables me to live . . . My breathing in is the sign of this . . . I give myself more and more to this reality . . . I open myself more and more completely to receive God's Spirit in the ground of my being . . . His Spirit flowing into me makes me fresh, strong, supple and kind . . . and enables me to bear fruit . . . I breathe in the Spirit of God . . . I am full of his Spirit.

9.   My breathing out also expresses a deep reality. I breathe out, giving myself away, relax in complete trust, die as I pour myself out and let myself go . . . This love is borne up by the life of God's

Spirit that has been present in me from baptism onwards . . . As I pour myself out in love I share more and more in the love that is poured into me . . . in the Holy Spirit who is living in me . . . I give myself completely to this process that is taking place in me . . . (see Rom 5. 5).

10.   The Spirit of God in me enables me to become more and more fully a child of this Father. This takes place on the one hand through love. Whoever loves, without relying simply on human love, will become a son of the Father in heaven (see Mt 5. 45). I desire more and more to learn how to love, drawing on this source, and how to live with this attitude . . . .. On the other hand, the face of Christ, my brother, becomes in this way more and more clearly expressed in me as the Spirit of Christ becomes more and more dominant in my life . . . My inner life is fashioned more and more closely in accordance with him . . . I am 'conformed to the image of the Son' (Rom 8. 29) . . . Christ is formed in me (see Gal 4. 19), expresses himself in me, becomes dominant in my life, lives in me . . . (see Phil 1. 21; Eph 3. 17; Gal 2. 20).

11.   I continue to meditate about my breathing as the symbol of God's love . . . I go a stage further in this meditation. Christ – the risen Christ who is now in the Spirit – lives in me . . . so that God's love does not simply come to me – it comes to Christ, who is mysteriously present in me . . . who lives in my thoughts, my senses, my believing and loving . . . and who in this way continues to live his life here on earth . . . Christ lives in me and I live in him. I reflect about this stream of love coming to me . . . I breathe it in . . . Breathing, I remain in this mystery of God's love and mercy. How shall I respond to it?

12.   Christ responds . . . It is his love, and his self-surrender to the Father, expressing itself, giving itself, giving itself away, losing itself in my breathing out . . . His life penetrates my life . . . His life brings me to life . . . I give myself entirely to meditation about this astonishing reality . . . It is the very centre of the world, the central act of the one who unites all things in heaven and on earth himself (Eph 1. 10), into which I have been drawn . . . I have been taken into Christ, who began this work on the cross . . . and who now lets his Church, those who belong to him, participate in his life . . . I breathe out, breathing out my life with him to God.

As the weeks and even the years go by, I come back again and again to this wonderful symbol of our relationship with God and of our life with God. Breathing — this is something that is always with me. It is a process by which I continue to live and to live with God. It is also an effective sign of my faith in God and of my way to salvation . . . While breathing, I also think of my fellow men and pray that they too will become increasingly filled with the Holy Spirit and the love of God.

30. In God — a testimony

If you have already made some progress in meditation, you may find this testimony useful in taking you to a deeper level. It may also serve to point the way to a reality to which we can and should open ourselves.

I had closed the door of my room and had sat down. I began to meditate, using the 'I am here' exercise.

I had reached the fifth stage in the exercise and the whole of my body was relaxed. I had let go of myself completely and was aware of myself in an attitude of total trust . . . I felt like a little child resting in its mother's arms . . .

In this state of complete trust, I opened myself irresistibly to the all-embracing mystery, the mystery that bears us up, accepts us, surrounds us and encloses us . . . I stayed quietly within this mystery . . . After a little while, I became conscious of the inner reality that the Son was living in me. The life of the Son deep within me . . . This life is adoration, openness and perfect self-surrender. I meditated for as long as possible about this reality and knew that what was present in me was the central act of the one who unites all things in the universe . . . Christ was in me . . . His life in me was flowing towards God . . .

31. Why I meditate

This text is not set out systematically. It originated as a testimony based on a number of questions. A few changes have been made in the original spontaneous statements.

I meditate
in order to find peace
and in order to enter the depths;
in order to find myself
and in order to live fully
and with all my strength.

I meditate
so that I do not become a desert within
and my inner sources do not dry up;
so that I do not simply live in a fragmentary way
and so that I can digest everything that I experience.

I meditate
to enable my everyday self and my deeper and essential
self to become one
and to enable the forces that are present in the depth of my being
to come to life;
to become free of all the unnecessary tensions imposed by the
world;
to learn how to be completely relaxed and recollected.

I meditate
to release the healing forces that are hidden within me;
to be made whole by living from the fulness and the depth
of my being.

I meditate
in order to become fully and truly human;
in order to become quite open and receptive to the people
and the things around me;
to have contact at the deepest level with my fellow men
and with myself
and to understand the meaning of my existence;
so that I will be able to experience at depth the fulness
of life given to me by God

and so that I will also come into contact with the
hidden riches of human existence and be sustained by it.

I meditate
because I hope that it will make me more sensitive to
what is essential
and more able to help other people;
because I want to be able to distinguish more clearly
what is really important for me and my fellow men
and to be more closely linked to them and to increase their
happiness and speak to them more intimately.

I meditate
in order to have a better understanding of God's intentions
and to become more and more an instrument in God's hands;
in order to overcome all resistance to his Spirit and his
Word.

I listen to what the Lord says to me in my innermost being
so that I will live more and more at the level of Holy
Scripture and understand more and more the meaning of
the Word of God;
so that the Spirit of Christ will become effective in me;
so that Jesus' words become alive for me and change my life;
so that I continue to change in accordance with the
process that probably began when I was a child
and so that things 'taste as they really are' for me.

I meditate
in order to expose myself more and more to God
who is 'at work in me, both to will and to work for his
good pleasure, (Phil 2. 13)
and to break down all the self-seeking barriers in me
that keep me from his will and his work.

I meditate
to give complete freedom to his Spirit;
to be open to receive Christ's joy and his peace

(Jn 15. 11: 'that my joy may be in you and that your joy
may be full'; 14. 27: 'peace I leave with you; my peace
I give you');
to be easily 'drawn' by him (see Jn 12. 32; 6. 44);
to be more receptive to the gifts of the Holy Spirit and
more completely filled with them ('love, joy, peace, patience,
kindness, goodness, faithfulness, gentleness and self-control',
Gal 5. 23)
and to achieve unity— unity within myself, unity with the
ultimate mystery and unity with all the many different things
and people I encounter . . .

I meditate
so that I will begin to understand the 'unsearchable riches
of Christ'(Eph 3. 8);
so that I will deepen my contacts with my fellow men — adults,
children and old people,
help them to find depth and fulness, riches and wholeness,
unity and recollection in their own existence
and in turn to spread this good news to other people.

I meditate
so that I shall no longer resist God's love;
so that I will learn how to surrender completely to him, not
merely externally, but in my innermost being;
so that I will be able to give myself up more and more fully
to the absolute demands of his love
and to eradicate even the most deeply concealed No to
God's will in my being.

I meditate
because I want to understand more and more 'what is the
breadth and length and height and depth' and 'to know the
love of Christ which surpasses knowledge' and, if it is
possible, 'to be filled with all the fulness of God' (Eph 3. 18-19);
because I want to leave behind all presumed independence and
isolation and enter the sphere of love, the life given to us by Christ
that does not end with death, but is fulfilled and consummated
beyond this life on earth

beyond this life on earth
and because I want above all to enjoy the experience in
which I no longer live – leading my petty, narrow, self-
seeking, presumptuous, shallow life without true peace
and fulfilment and exposed to emotion and desires – but in
which Christ lives more and more in me (Gal 2. 20: 'It is
no longer I who live, but Christ who lives in me').

I would also like to play a small part
in helping the people of God to find their true source
and, together with other Christian believers, I look
forward to the fulfilment of the promise: 'What no eye
has seen, nor ear heard, nor the heart of man conceived,
what God has prepared for those who love him' (1 Cor 2. 9).

I know too
that meditation is prayer
that transcends words and even thoughts and aspirations
and that this may be what Jesus meant when he said that
we ought always to pray and not lose heart (Lk 18. 1).

I meditate
so that we shall be able to pass through the tribulations
ahead with endurance and faith (see Rev 13. 10).

I meditate also
because it is the beginning of the eternal life in which we
contemplate God

and I meditate finally
because it is true that no painter ever painted a picture,
no poet ever wrote a poem, no man ever became a true man
and no Christian ever became a real Christian without meditation.

32. The 'You' song (Martin Buber)

> Wherever I go — You
> Wherever I am — You
> Only You, always You.
> You, You, You.
> If life is going well — You
> If I am suffering — You
> You, You, always You.
> You, You, You.
> Heaven — You,
> Earth — You
> above — You
> below — You
> Wherever I turn,
> only You, always You.
> You, You, You.